"Is Our Children Learning?"

—George W. Bush, Grand Rapids, Michigan, January 11, 2000[1]

The Case Against George W. Bush

Paul Begala

Simon & Schuster

New York • London • Toronto • Sydney • Singapore

SIMON & SCHUSTER
Rockefeller Center
1230 Avenue of the Americas
New York, NY 10020

Copyright © 2000 by Paul Begala

Designed by Lisa Chovnick

Manufactured in the United States of America

3   5   7   9   10   8   6   4   2

Library of Congress Cataloging-in-Publication Data is available.

ISBN 0-7432-1478-1
ISBN 13: 978-0-7432-1478-0

Acknowledgments

I could never have written this book without Mary Matalin. Mrs. James Carville is so loyal to her old pal George W. Bush that she threatened to leave James if he took up Simon & Schuster's offer to write this book. So James, the best friend a guy ever had and the most brilliant political mind of our time, suggested me to David Rosenthal of Simon & Schuster. Their faith in me is deeply appreciated.

The meticulous documentation and factual accuracy of this book are entirely due to the hard work of Doug Kelly and his remarkable staff of researchers at the Democratic National Committee. Like me, they believe politics should be fought—and fought hard—on the battlefield of issues and ideas, not rumor and innuendo like some on the right. Every page of this book reflects their zeal for accuracy, and I am grateful for their tremendous contributions of research, analysis, and writing. Still, whatever errors there may be in this book are mine and mine alone.

Jon Macks offered one-liners and encouragement in great abundance. He is a true friend and either the funniest smart person I know or the smartest funny person I know. Bob Barnett once again proved to be a good friend and consigliere, and my friend Mark Weiner offered both marketing advice and moral support. Geoff Kloske of Simon & Schuster proved an able and expeditious editor.

Many of the absurd and revealing quotations from Governor Bush contained herein were first compiled and published by Jacob Weisberg of Slate.com. His "Bushisms" are priceless, and updated each week. Keep 'em coming, Jacob.

Molly Ivins and Lou Dubose have done a great public service in writing *Shrub: The Short but Happy Political Life of George W. Bush.* I leaned heavily on their work in my summary of Bush's career in the Texas oil business.

Steve Lewis, the executive producer of my show, *Equal Time* (6:30 P.M. Eastern on MSNBC), and the entire MSNBC gang (Jeff Kepnes, Kerri Forrest, Jennifer Weems, Liliana Lopez, Rick Murphy, Cara Kennedy, and all the rest) have been supportive to the point of indulgence. And even my on-air adversary, Ollie North, helped make this book better (albeit unwittingly) by sharpening my points in the heat of political combat.

My family put up with the late nights and grouchy days that went into producing this book. My mother, Peggy Howard, read the first draft and offered much needed encouragement. And my sister, Kathleen, contributed both good ideas and priceless baby-sitting services. My boys, John, Billy, Charlie, and Patrick (who was born as I was writing this book), provided all the inspiration, hugs, laughs, and baseball-playing breaks a dad could want.

Of course, like every good thing in my life, I owe this most of all to my wife, Diane.

For Diane

— the beautiful, brilliant girl I met in the

Geography Building at the University of Texas

nearly twenty years ago, the gorgeous,

brilliant woman today — who

produced a miracle named Patrick Aaron

as I was hacking away at this book.

Contents

"Is
Our
Children
Learning?"

Introduction

At first I really liked George W. Bush.

Having grown up mostly in Texas, I left in 1989 to become a political consultant in Washington, D.C. Because I had the good sense to partner up with James Carville, I had a run of good luck, helping elect such Democrats as Governor Bob Casey of Pennsylvania (who died, sadly, this year), Governor (now Senator) Zell Miller of Georgia, and Senators Frank Lautenberg of New Jersey and Harris Wofford of Pennsylvania.

Then, in 1992, Carville and I served as senior strategists for the Clinton-Gore campaign. It was like being the jockey on Secretariat. Clinton and Gore won, and Carville and I went on to fame and fortune. But by 1995 the Republicans had taken over Congress, and Dick Morris had largely taken over Carville's and my role as principal political adviser. And since my wife and I were expecting our second baby, I had no desire to leave my growing family for another long campaign.

So I returned to my beloved Texas in 1995, Bush's first year as governor. I met him, and he impressed me. I thought then—and I think now—that he's a basically good man. He seems to have an abiding faith in God—and in himself—and an intense devotion to his family, his state, and our nation. And he's not a bigot. (If this seems like damning with faint praise to you, I'm not kidding. Most of the success the Republican party has enjoyed in the South is directly attributable to the Democratic party's support for—and the GOP's opposition to—racial equality.) Bush truly doesn't know the meaning of the word "intolerance." (But then again, he doesn't know what continent Mexico is on, the name of the prime minister of India, or where he was for a year in the National Guard. But that's for later in this book.)

So to encounter a successful Southern Republican who didn't seem to have an ounce of prejudice in him was a delight. I went out of my way to say nice things about him, and he reciprocated. We exchanged complimentary notes, and I was perfectly happy to praise him in the press—especially when he tried to raise taxes in order to improve school funding. (He failed.) I even described his early years in office as "an unqualified success." But as a potential president I can only give him half that description: unqualified.

What's changed? Two things: I learned more about Bush (and how easily I could fall for first impressions), and Bush decided that he wanted to be our president.

I still think Bush is a basically decent guy. But I'm deeply troubled by much of what he has done and what he has failed to do—in business and as governor of Texas—and I am flat-out petrified about him becoming our president.

President Clinton lured me back to Washington to serve as one of his top White House aides in 1997. In that job I had a front-row seat from which to study the American presidency. Clinton, despite his personal failings, is the smartest person I've ever known and the most talented politician I've ever seen. And the job took every bit of his intellect; it demanded every ounce of his talent. On top of all that, the job required every iota of Clinton's vaunted compassion. Not the stuff of Bush's platitudinous speeches; the real thing. The kind of empathy that knew instinctively what to do when an elderly woman in New Hampshire collapsed sobbing in his arms as she tried to tell him how she had to choose between paying to heat her home or for her prescription drugs.

W, you're going to hate me when someone reads this to you. (I know you're not big on books yourself.) But you don't have what it takes to be president. Even your most loyal defenders say you're a few beans shy of a full burrito intellectually. And your whole career has been a case study in the art of failing upward. You were a poor student who somehow got into the finest schools. You were a National Guardsman who somehow disappeared from duty for a year. You were a failed businessman who somehow got rich. You were a minority investor who somehow was made managing partner of the Texas Rangers baseball team. And you were a defeated politician who somehow was made governor.

Let's face it, Dub: you were born on third base, and you think you hit a triple. You're lighter than my grandma's biscuits. You know it. I know it. And now the American people are going to know it.

This book examines the real record of George Walker Bush: a man who presents the thinnest, weakest, least impressive record in public life of any major party nominee for the presidency this century. A man who at every critical juncture has been propelled upward by the forces of wealth, privilege, status, and special interests who would use his family's name for their private gain.

But before we start, a brief word about what this book is not. It is not a product of the Gore for President campaign. In fact, with the exception of my sister (who used to be Gore's communications director) I didn't even tell anyone from the Gore campaign I was writing this book. Nor is this book a sales job on why you should vote for Al Gore for president. I am fully qualified to write such a book, having worked with him in the 1992 campaign and served with him in the White House. The Al Gore I know has the quality of mind, the depth of spirit, the firmness of principle, and the goodness of heart to be a great president. But I don't flack for Al Gore. He can make the case for his candidacy just fine without me.

This book is prompted by my own experience as a partisan, as a political analyst, as a strategist, and as a Texan observing Bush. It is not a hatchet job. It is meticulously documented. (For my right-wing friends who get their news from AM radio blowhards, those little numbers are notes; scholars use them to authenticate their work.) And it is limited to Bush's public life and public record. I have no interest or desire to poke around in Bush's private life, nor do I particularly care if he had too many beers at a college kegger, or experimented with something worse twenty-five years ago. This is not the politics of personal destruction. It is documentation of Bush's brand of politics: the politics of platitudes, the politics of cynical sound bites devoid of substance, the politics of familial vengeance, and the politics of faithfully serving the interests of those who have made you wealthy and powerful.

I have looked behind W's smirk. This is what I found.

chapter 1

Governor Bush: My Substitute Teacher

"The most important job is not to be governor, or first lady in my case."

(San Antonio Express-News, 1/30/00)

"He hasn't really done much as a governor in regards of doing anything new or innovative."

(Republican governor Tommy Thompson of Wisconsin, Associated Press, 2/19/99)

To understand how ludicrous it is for George W. Bush to claim that his time as governor of Texas has prepared him for the White House, consider this story:

Back in 1996 I was teaching at the University of Texas at Austin. The course was called "Politics and the Press" and I taught it alongside the veteran Austin journalist and all-around great guy Dave McNeely. During the presidential campaign of 1996, Bill Clinton and Al Gore (for whom I had worked in 1992) asked me to help them prepare for the debates. Naturally, I was thrilled to do so. But there was one problem: I needed a substitute teacher. The premise of the course was for a longtime reporter and a political professional to compare notes across the divide between reporters and politicians, so I needed a pol. McNeely invited Karen Hughes, the press secretary for Governor Bush, and I went off to debate prep knowing that my class would be ably covered.

When I returned I learned that on her way out the door, Hughes had mentioned to Bush that she was going to be a guest lecturer, and Bush asked her if he could go as well. And so George W. Bush served as my substitute teacher.

The students liked him. They found him to be charming and disarming. The consensus was he'd been a pretty good substitute teacher. But you wouldn't give him his own class: the job's too big for him.

There are a couple of lessons you can learn from this story:

1. That Bush is a nice guy who was open and accessible to students;

2. That Bush is a nice guy who was open and accessible to students because he really doesn't have anything to do as governor.

You see, the governor of Texas is not like other governors. He has no power. None. I mean, aside from signing or vetoing bills and nominating people for the myriad state boards and commissions, he's got nothing to do. That's how we Texans want it. We have what the political scientists call "a weak governor system." And in that weak governor system, Bush fits right in. He's weaker than rainwater.

The governor of Texas doesn't have a cabinet. He doesn't write the budget. He doesn't run the state bureaucracy or manage the state's finances. The governor of Texas doesn't run anything bigger than his mouth. It's a job made to order for Ol' W. He looks the part, shows up, gives an appropriately vapid speech, cuts the ribbon, shoots the bull, then is whisked away to the next phony-baloney photo op with the Queen of the Luling Watermelon Thump.

The governorship in Texas is ceremonial. "The lieutenant-governor presides over the state senate, chairs the board that writes the budget and is more powerful than the governor," according to Nicholas Lemann of *The New Yorker.* "Though the second biggest state in the union, only 137 people report to W. To give you a sense of contrast, the Arkansas governor has 1,400 and the mayor of Chicago about 42,000."[1]

So the governor has very little work to do, and lots of time to kill. So what does the governor do all day? Well, he works—for three and a half hours—from 8:00 A.M. to 11:30 A.M., then takes three and a half hours of personal time to jog, nap, read, and have lunch[2] and play video golf or computer solitaire until 3:00 P.M.[3] Then it's back to the grind—straight through till 5:00 or 5:30.

Whew. I don't know how the man does it.

But Bush, bless his heart, seems to think that's what the presidency is all about, too. Of course you, dear reader, know better, because you probably read that civics textbook in high school. You know that the American presidency is the most difficult, demanding, complicated, intricate, and exhausting job in the world. Why on earth would we give it to a guy whose only qualification is being nice enough to substitute-teach for me?

The governor of Texas has little real power, but he *can* provide a moral example. And Bush loves to give pious, pontificating lectures about just how moral he is. One of W's favorite applause lines is that he will "restore honor and integrity to the Oval Office." When I first heard it, I figured he was referring to the terrible lack of integrity his father showed by lying to the country about his role in Iran-Contra. But then my Bushie friends told me he was referring to the fact that President Clinton had an affair and lied about it. Now, I think having an affair—and lying about it—is wrong. But I also think selling deadly missiles to the Ayatollah and lying about it is wrong.

But what's different, the Bushies say, is that Clinton lied under oath. Well, W was caught up in a similar game of legalistic "gotcha." In a lawsuit about whether Bush's staff had blocked an investigation of a funeral home corporation that had given Bush thousands of dollars, Bush swore under oath that he never had any "conversations" about the investigation with anyone at the corporation or the agency investigating it. But a lobbyist for the company and the chair of the agency both contradicted Bush in public statements. The lobbyist said Bush stuck his head in a meeting of the lobbyist, the head of the company, and Bush's chief of staff and asked if the agency was "still messing with you?" In fact, Bush himself publicly contradicted his own sworn statement. He offered a tortured, hairsplitting explanation of why he hadn't really lied under oath. Apparently W thinks it depends on what the meaning of "conversation" is. According to the AP he said, "It's a twenty-second conversation. I had no substantive conversation with the guy. Twenty seconds. That's hardly enough time to even say hello, much less sit down and have a substantive discussion. . . . I can't remember what I said. All I know is it lasted no time."[4]

chapter 2

Where's George? How Bush Disappeared from the National Guard for a Year

[After completing flight training in 1970] "I continued flying with my unit for the next several years."

> (George W. Bush in his autobiography,
> *A Charge to Keep,* as quoted in the *Boston Globe,* 5/23/00)

"Had he reported in, I would have had some recall, and I do not. I had been in Texas, done my flight training there. If we had had a first lieutenant from Texas, I would have remembered."

> (General William Turnipseed, commander of the Alabama National Guard unit to which Bush had been assigned, *Boston Globe,* 5/23/00)

Think back to the days of the war in Vietnam. (If you're too young to remember them, think back to *Apocalypse Now.*) Because of the absurdly elitist rules governing the draft, the sons of working people are being shipped off to Vietnam by the thousands, while the sons of the powerful and the privileged remain safe at home.

But one son of privilege decides to do his duty. Although deeply conflicted about the war his father in Congress is opposing, he volunteers for the army. Despite his Ivy League education he enlists as a grunt, a lowly private, and ships out for Vietnam. That gutsy young man was Al Gore. This is not his story.

This is the story of another son of privilege and power, another Ivy League–educated man who, although not at all conflicted about the war his father in Congress was supporting, does not enlist in the army and ship out for Vietnam. He enlists in the Texas Air National Guard. He is George W. Bush.

In fairness to W, this is dangerous duty. He wants to be a pilot, and pilots die in training with tragic frequency. So you'll get no sneering from me about Bush's service in the Guard.

It's his lack of service that bothers mo.

Friends in High Places: How Bush Got in the Guard in the First Place

Back in 1968, being in the National Guard was a coveted ticket out of getting your ass shot off in Vietnam. Despite a waiting list of 500, Bush was vaulted to the head of the line. He only scored in the 25th percentile in the pilot aptitude test,[1] yet he was approved for an automatic commission as a second lieutenant and assigned to flight school, a role usually reserved for young men with ROTC or air force experience. Bush had neither.[2]

Both Bush and his father deny they asked for preferential treatment, although such treatment was common for the sons of the wealthy and powerful. And then–Texas House Speaker Ben Barnes has testified under oath that he did in fact pull strings to get W into the Texas Air National Guard, "at the request of a businessman from Houston named Sid Adger." Adger lived in the same Midland neighborhood and attended the same clubs as the Bush family while George W. was growing up. However, Barnes said that Adger gave no indication that the call came at the Bushes' urging.[3]

"Favorable Treatment and Uncommon Attention"

Once he got in the Guard, W's run of good luck continued. According to the *Los Angeles Times,* "An examination of nearly 200 pages of his service record obtained by the *Times,* plus interviews with Guard officials, veterans, and military experts, show that Bush, now 52 and governor of Texas, received favorable treatment and uncommon attention in his time in the Guard."[4]

Despite the preferential treatment, most accounts of Bush's days in the Texas Air National Guard show him to be a good pilot who took his work seriously and performed his service honorably. Then in the fall of 1972, things changed. Bush wanted to work for the Senate campaign of Alabama Republican Winton "Red" Blount, Richard Nixon's former postmaster general. Bush asked for and received a transfer to the Alabama Guard. His request was approved even though the comparable unit in Alabama was being phased out. The *Los Angeles Times* noted that with the Alabama unit downsizing, "there appeared to be no real task for [Bush] to perform."[5]

Here's where the plot thickens, and the Bush doo-doo gets deep:

Where's George?

Bush didn't show up for duty in Alabama. At least that's what the records say. That's what the commanding officer says. That's what the administrative officer says. But that's not what Bush says. Let us walk through this morass carefully:

On September 5, 1972, First Lieutenant George W. Bush was ordered to report to the 187th Tactical Region Group of the Alabama Air National Guard in Montgomery. He was directed to report to the commanding officer, General William Turnipseed.[6]

But General Turnipseed says he never showed. "Had he reported in," the general told the *Boston Globe*, "I would have had some recall, and I do not. I had been in Texas, done my flight training there. If we had had a first lieutenant from Texas, I would have remembered."[7]

The general's administrative officer, Kenneth K. Lott, backs him up. Lott says that he, too, has no recollection of Bush ever reporting for duty. And even retired Colonel Albert Lloyd, a longtime Texas Air National Guard official who is otherwise full of praise for Bush and his service, had to admit to the *Globe* that he doesn't know if Bush fulfilled his duty in Alabama. "If he did," Colonel Lloyd said, "his drill attendance should have been certified and sent to Ellington [the Texas airbase from which Bush had been transferred], and there would have been a record. We cannot find the records to show he fulfilled the requirements in Alabama."[8] And, as the *Globe*'s investigation pointed out, Bush's discharge papers have no record of any service whatsoever in Alabama, and no record of any service for an entire year. "There should have been an entry for the period between May 1972 and May 1973," Lloyd told the *Globe*.[9]

So, where was George? I have no idea. But it is stunning that after months of effort, the Bush campaign cannot produce a single person who can personally vouch for Bush's service in Alabama. The Bushies did produce a woman who said she was seeing Bush socially at the time, and he had told her he had to hurry back for Guard duty.[10] But if girlfriends are now the proof of military service, my old boss Bill Clinton should get the Congressional Medal of Honor.

Bush cannot say what he was doing. "I can't remember what I did," he told a press conference.[11] Expanding on Bush's remarks, campaign senior adviser Ari Fleischer quoted Bush as saying he did "paper shuffling" in Montgomery. "He thinks it was desk work," said Fleischer.[12] "Governor Bush specifically remembers pulling duty in Alabama at the end of the campaign," says Dan Bartlett, another spokesman.[13] And at another time, Bartlett suggested the work was that all-important "odds and ends."

(I remember exactly what I was doing at the end of 1972 and the beginning of 1973: going to the sixth grade at John Foster Dulles Junior High School in Sugar Land, Texas. In our ultraconservative little town we were taught about old-fashioned values of duty and honor and country. They never mentioned that rich people could take a walk on those values if they became inconvenient. They must have covered that ground for Bush at his elite private boarding school, Andover.)

Bush cannot say for whom he was doing whatever it was he was doing. His spokesman says he worked under different supervisors whose names he does not recall.[14]

He hasn't named a single person he served with in Alabama. In fact, as the Associated Press reported, "Gov. George W. Bush's campaign workers have concluded that no documents exist showing he reported for duty as ordered in Alabama with the Texas Air National Guard in 1972."[15] And Bush's claim that he may have made up the time upon returning to Ellington Air Force Base in Texas is refuted by the unit's former administrative officer.[16]

But we know what he was *not* doing. Reporting for his flight physical. And he's given a variety of excuses as to why.

- The "My Doctor Lives in a Different City" Excuse:
  According to the *Los Angeles Times*, "A Bush spokesman said that this [missing the exam] occurred because Bush was in Alabama while his physician was in Houston." (*Los Angeles Times*, 7/4/99)

- "The Paperwork Hasn't Caught Up Yet" Excuse:
  Bush spokesman Dan Bartlett told the *Sunday Times* of London that Bush was aware at the time that he would be suspended for missing his medical exam, but had no choice because he had applied for a transfer from Houston to Alabama and his paperwork hadn't caught up with him. "It was just a question of following the bureaucratic procedure of the time," Bartlett said. "He knew the suspension would have to take place." (*New York Post*, 6/18/00)

- The "There Was No Reason for the Exam" Excuse:
  Dan Bartlett said Bush had transferred to Alabama as a nonflying guardsman and so required no medical assessment. "As he was not flying, there was no reason for him to take the flight exam," said Bartlett. "And he was not aware of any changes that required a drug test." (*Sunday Times* of London, 6/18/00)

The Bottom Line

I don't believe Bush. Call me skeptical, but I'm going with the word of a retired general (and I'm just guessing that a retired general from Alabama is not a raving leftist), a couple of colonels, and hundreds of pages of records. With the exception of Bush's implausible denials, the record here is quite clear: Bush avoided going to Vietnam by securing a coveted spot in the Texas Air National Guard. While stationed in Texas he performed hazardous duty honorably. But when he requested and received his transfer to Alabama, he did little or nothing to fulfill his duty. The fact that he was honorably discharged only means that he got away with it.

Back in the Second World War, a little private from Detroit didn't show up for duty. His father was not a powerful congressman, and his grandfather had not been a senator. His family did not have a majestic mansion on the surf-pounded cliffs of Kennebunkport. Private Eddie Slovik deserted. And Eddie Slovik was shot by a firing squad.

Thus proving once more the enduring lesson of W's life: it's good to be a Bush.

I'm not accusing Bush of desertion, mind you. He was not on active duty, much less in combat. But it's pretty clear that the man who pontificates about how, when he takes the oath of office as president, he will "restore honor and dignity to the presidency" did not fulfill his oath of office as a first lieutenant in the Texas Air National Guard.

chapter 3

El Busto: Bush as a Bidnessman

"I understand small business growth. I was one."

(New York Daily News, 2/19/00)

"Nobody has ever said that George is an outstanding brain, or some great risk-taker."

(Businessman Paul Rea, who worked with George W. Bush in the oil business, *Dallas Morning News*, 7/30/99)

Given how little the governor of Texas can do—and how badly Governor Bush has done it—it's no wonder Bush is touting his record as a businessman. But for Bush to claim he's been a success in business is like one of those early NASA chimps claiming he flew in outer space. He may have been along for the ride, but his hands weren't exactly on the wheel.

In the private sector, Bush has always been more of a front man than a bidnessman (that's how we say it in Texas). Bush's greatest gift in business has always been his name; his greatest talent his utterly shameless willingness to trade on that family name.

Bush graduated from the Harvard Business School with a master's in Business Administration in 1975. But by his own admission, he spent much of his time after graduation "drinking and carousing and fumbling around."[1] By 1977, he started his first company, Arbusto Energy, Inc. "Arbusto" is Spanish for "bush." Apparently W is willing to trade on his family name in a bilingual fashion. You get the feeling that if Bush had wanted to do business in China, he would have named the company "Lien"—which is Chinese for "bush." [2]

But while Arbusto was incorporated in 1977, it did not begin operations until 1979. Why? Bush created the company on the eve of his run for Congress, where he was trying to represent oil-soaked Midland, Texas. Creating Arbusto allowed Bush to be described (inaccurately) as "a thirty-two-year-old Midland oil producer" when in fact Arbusto had not produced anything but a paper filing. [3]

(By the way, by 1978 Al Gore, although two years younger than Bush, had already volunteered for the army and served on active duty in Vietnam, spent five years as a reporter, including uncovering corruption on Nashville's city council, run for Congress and won, and co-sponsored the resolution that allowed television and radio coverage of congressional proceedings.)

But back to Arbusto. In March 1979, just months after losing his congressional race, Bush and Arbusto began active operations. That is to say Bush started actively shaking down his Poppy's rich friends and relatives for start-up money. Yes, this small bidnessman, this bold and courageous entrepreneur, just happened to have the rare talent of raising $4.7 million from some of the wealthiest and most powerful financiers on the East Coast, including George L. Ball, the CEO of Prudential Bache Securities, Lewis Lehrman, who once ran against Mario Cuomo for governor of New York, a guy with the Gatsbyesque name of FitzGerald Bemiss, who'd known Poppy all his life and who is godfather to W's brother Marvin. One investor described the folks who funded W as "All the Bushes' pals. This is the A-Team." [4] How did he do it? Is W some kind of idiot savant, unable to finish a sentence in the English language, but possessed of rare and special business acumen?

As Molly Ivins and Lou Dubose point out in their excellent book, *Shrub: The Short but Happy Political Life of George W. Bush,* the vast majority of the millions Bush raised for Arbusto was ponied up while another man named George Bush just happened to be one of the most powerful politicians in America: running for president, and later serving as vice president. Arbusto drilled its first well in 1979. It was a dry hole, the first of many. "The first well I ever drilled in which I had a participatory interest was dry," Bush later recalled. "And I'll never forget the feeling. Kind of 'Oops. This is not quite as easy as we all thought it was going to be.' "[5]

Kind of "Oops" indeed. Arbusto was so badly run by Bush that folks in the oil patch called it "El Busto," and indeed Bush lost millions of dollars of other people's money.[6] But you know what they say: there's nothing better than "opium"—Other People's Money.

Bush ran El Busto into the ground. But his investors seemed happy. In part that's because special-interest tax breaks allowed them in some cases to write off as much as 91 percent of the capital invested in some of the projects.[7]

It was in 1982 that Bush once more demonstrated his unique talent for finding sugar daddies. As Ivins and Dubose point out in *Shrub,* Philip Uzielli, the CEO of Panamanian-based Executive Resources, purchased a 10 percent stake in Bush's company. Now, here's the mathematics portion of our little book. Don't worry, even if you skipped school as often as W, you can get this one.

El Busto at the time had a book value of $382,376, according to financial statements cited by Ivins and Dubose.[8] What's 10 percent of a $382,376 company worth? Take your time. Think about it. Feel free to use a calculator if you want. You can even use a lifeline to call a friend.

Okay, time's up. If you said a 10 percent stake in a $382,376 company should be worth in the range of $38,237.60, you're right. Unless your daddy's vice president. 'Cause W sold that same 10 percent share to Mr. Uzielli for a cool $1 million.[9]

How did Bush sell something worth around thirty-eight grand for a million bucks? Of course, the Boy Genius is too modest—and too canny—to let us in on his secret. "A company balance sheet can be misleading" was his Forrest Gumpian comment afterward.[10]

After Poppy became vice president, W made another bold move. The kind of move only the savviest, smartest, most canny bidnessman could have come up with.

He changed the company's name.

Apparently worried that those who wanted to suck up to Vice President Poppy by bailing out his goofball son might be confused by the Spanish name Arbusto, W renamed the company Bush Exploration in 1982.[11] Bush Exploration was not exactly Exxon. According to the industry research group Petroleum Information Corp., Bush Exploration operated a grand total of sixteen oil wells, making it the 993rd largest oil company in Texas.[12] But it had one hell of an asset: its name. Apparently that was enough for the sugar daddies who wanted to suck up to Bush's daddy. But it wasn't enough for the public. When W tried to sell shares in his company on the open market, he'd hoped to raise $6 million. He only came away with $1.1 million.[13] Why do you suppose W was so successful in raising money for his failed ventures from some of the smartest businessmen in the world, yet couldn't sell shares to mom-and-pop investors? Could it have something to do with the fact that your mom and pop were in no position to cash in on Bush's Poppy? Naaaah. Probably just a further testament to the prescient powers of the elite investors. They know a loss-leader can sometimes reap huge returns down the road.

The story gets murkier from here, and if you want all the details, I highly recommend Molly Ivins and Lou Dubose's book, the aforementioned *Shrub*. But here are some of the highlights:

- **1983:** Bush sells Bush Exploration to an outfit called Spectrum 7, run by Mercer Reynolds III and William O. DeWitt, Jr.[14] Reflecting back on W's involvement, DeWitt said Bush was not known for making gut-wrenching decisions. "I can't remember any," says Mr. DeWitt.[15]

- **1986:** Harken Energy buys Spectrum 7. "We didn't have a fair price for oil, but we had George," said Harken director E. Stuart Watson. "And George was very useful to Harken. . . . As far as contacts were concerned, he was terrific. . . . It seemed like George knew everybody in the U.S. who was worth knowing."[16]

- **1989:** Bush is allowed to purchase 1.8 percent of the Texas Rangers baseball team. He has no experience in sports management, but is made managing partner. He trades Sammy Sosa.[17]

- **1989:** Some guy named George Bush is inaugurated president of the United States of America.

- **1989:** As *Time* magazine later described it, officials of the oil-rich Persian Gulf nation of Bahrain "suddenly and mysteriously broke off promising talks with Amoco" (the oil giant) and instead turn their attention, and their lucrative drilling contract, to Harken Energy.[18]

- **1990:** Harken Energy lands a lucrative and exclusive contract to drill for oil in the Persian Gulf nation of Bahrain. Harken had never before drilled for oil overseas. "It was a surprise," an industry analyst tells *Time* magazine. "Harken is not traditionally a company that explores internationally."[19]

- **1990:** A Palestinian-born investor named Talat Othman gains remarkable access to the Bush White House, garnering no fewer than three White House meetings with President Bush to discuss the Middle East. By sheer coincidence, Othman serves on the board of Harken Energy, representing Sheik Abdullah Bakhsh of Saudi Arabia, who owns 17.6 percent of Harken's stock.[20] The *Wall Street Journal* writes, "Mr. Othman's political access coincides with the remarkable ascendance of a little Texas oil company on whose board he serves alongside George W. Bush, the president's oldest son."[21]

- **May 1990:** According to "an informed source" quoted in *U.S. News & World Report,* Harken Energy's creditors had threatened to foreclose; Harken's treasurer denies it. Smith Barney warns Bush and other senior Harken officials that only extreme measures can salvage the situation.[22]

- **June 1990:** Bush once again displays his remarkable brilliance, pulling off a business deal that you and I could never have done—because you and I weren't insiders in Harken Energy. Bush sells two thirds of his stock in Harken Energy. The public has no way of knowing that the company is in what Poppy would call "deep doo-doo," so W sells his shares for $848,560, or $4 a share, "at almost the top of the market," according to the *Wall Street Journal.* Once losses are reported, just two months after Bush bailed, the stock falls to $2.37 a share, before finally bottoming out at $1 by the end of 1990. Bush was a director of the company, a consultant to the company, and a member of its audit committee.[23] *U.S. News & World Report* says there was "substantial evidence to suggest Bush knew Harken was in dire straits."[24] As an insider, Bush was legally obligated to report the stock sale immediately. Instead he fails to file the legally mandatory disclosure documents until eight months past their deadline.[25]

- **1991:** Led by George W. Bush, the Texas Rangers con the good people of Arlington, Texas, into raising their taxes to build Bush and his partners a stadium. The deal is a curious blend of the worst of socialism and capitalism: the government puts up the money, thereby socializing the downside risk, but Bush and his cronies make the profit, thereby privatizing the upside reward.

- **1998:** Bush (who is by now governor of Texas) and his partners sell the Texas Rangers. Largely because of the value of the tax-payer-funded stadium, and generous partners who have increased Bush's share of the team from less than 2 percent to almost 12 percent without requiring him to invest any more money, Bush makes a killing. His original $606,000 investment nets him a return of $14.9 million.

The Bottom Line

So what have we learned about George W. Bush the bidnessman? That his many critics sell him short. Again and again we see a man with the Midas touch. A man who can turn nothing but a trust fund and a willingness to cash in on his family name into an enormous fortune. Let's face it: he's a genius. How else can you explain the Chauncey Gardiner–like success of a man who failed in the oil patch, failed as a baseball executive, and walked away with a fortune so vast it's unlikely his children will ever have to work for a living?

chapter 4

Bush's Emphasis on Education: Public Policy, or a Desperate Cry for Help?

"I said, 'No, we're not going to take your Goals 2000 money. There are too many strings. I can't cite you the strings. I was just told that there were too many strings.' And so I said no."

(Bush, recounting his answer to an offer
from the Clinton administration to send a
package of education funds to Texas, C-SPAN, 1/25/99)

"Higher education is not my priority."

(*San Antonio Express-News*, 3/22/98)

"Laura and I sometimes don't realize how bright our children is until we get an objective analysis."

(*Meet the Press*, 4/15/00)

"Reading is the basics for all learning."

(Reston, Virginia, 3/28/00)

"How do you know if you don't measure up if you have a system that simply suckles kids through?"

(Hilton Head, South Carolina, 2/16/00)

"Governor Bush will not stand for the subsidation of failure."

(Speaking of himself in the third person,
Florence, South Carolina, 1/11/00)

It is ironic that a guy who never went to class, was a crummy student, and boasts of his anti-intellectual grievances should choose education as his top issue. Kind of like Rush Limbaugh giving diet tips—sure, it's an important problem; but is this really the guy to solve it?

Let's be honest. If you want to hide something from George W. Bush, put it in a book. He has all the intellectual curiosity of a slug, combined with the goofy, geeky syntactical spasms of his father.

He went to some of the best schools in the world: Andover, Yale, Harvard. (By the way, how did he get into those schools? He was the last of the legacies—a beneficiary of affirmative action for the overprivileged children of the Eastern elite aristocracy.) But he doesn't seem to have learned a damn thing. And he seems proud of that. Defiant ignorance has been his approach to his own education. Why should we put him in charge of our kids'?

In fairness to W, education is the only policy area you can talk to him about, in which his eyes don't look like a slot machine hitting BAR-APPLE-LEMON. But it strikes me as odd that a guy like Bush, who just oozes contempt for all things intellectual, would choose to apply his teeny, tiny brain to the issue of education. That's his right, of course. Just like the guy who played Mini-Me in *Austin Powers* has a right to try out for the Olympic basketball team. We just don't expect much in the way of results. And if the team wins, folks will know it was in spite of him, not because of him.

There's a famous logical fallacy—so popular it was even used by the president played by Martin Sheen on *The West Wing*—*post hoc, ergo propter hoc*. (It's Latin, Governor, get Karl Rove, your chief strategist, to explain it to you. No, not Italian, *Latin*.) It means "after that, therefore because of that." The classic example is the rooster taking credit for the dawn. Or W taking credit for educational improvements in Texas. Let's look at the real record.

The Most Important Reforms Were in Place
Before Bush Became Governor

There's a wonderful story about a young man who wanted to be a walk-on during the glory days of Texas Longhorn football. He confidently strode up to Coach Darrell Royal and declared, "Coach, you've got to put me on the team. I can run the forty in four seconds flat." Royal was impressed. "Really?" he asked. "And that's not all. I can also throw the ball seventy-five yards on a dead spiral, and I've never missed a field goal within fifty yards."

By now Coach Royal was astounded—but skeptical. "Every football player has his weakness," he said. "What's yours, son?" And the young man said, "Well, Coach, I do tend to exaggerate."

When W talks about education, he reminds me of that boastful young man. Eager to impress, wanting to be taken seriously. And completely full of bull. Education reform in Texas predates Bush's tenure as governor by a decade. Back in 1984, Democratic governor Mark White made education reform his top priority. He appointed Ross Perot to chair a special commission on education reform, and—bless Ross's crazy little Martian heart—he enacted the most sweeping education reforms in Texas history. The White-Perot reforms included a mandatory reduction in class size to twenty-two students per class in grades kindergarten through four, competency testing for teachers, and the controversial "No-Pass, No-Play," which barred failing students from extracurricular activities.[1]

The Fort Worth Star-Telegram looked into all this, and concluded:

> A review of the record indicates that the state's most important school reforms—including standardized tests and other accountability measures—took root long before Bush moved into the Governor's Mansion. Education experts, and even Bush aides, say that his predecessors are more responsible for improvements in Texas education.[2]

So Bush is not responsible for the reductions in class size. In fact, he called for effectively eliminating the limit on class size as an infringement of local control.[3] He's not responsible for the accountability tests, which had their origins a decade before him, and were fully implemented in 1994, when Ann Richards was governor.[4] And he's not responsible for "No-Pass, No-Play."

But he is responsible for the state budget. When he was running for office, Bush promised to increase the state's share of public school funding from 45 percent to 60 percent. After five years, the state's share of public school funding has actually dropped to 44.3 percent.[5]

So what the hell is W crowing about?

"Higher Education Is Not My Priority."

The state has a fine university system. (Full disclosure: I'm a graduate of Texas' public schools and the University of Texas at Austin and UT Law, which, by the way, turned W down for admission because it operated on a merit system for admission. But don't cry for him, Argentina, he got into Harvard Business School, which back then admitted on the incestuous "legacy" policy, not merit.) Perhaps because he was turned down by UT, Bush has been downright hostile to higher education in Texas. As the *Chronicle of Higher Education* said, "For Mr. Bush, who boasts in stump speeches that he is a 'reformer with results,' the needs of the state's colleges and universities have never been a top issue. A common response by college officials when asked about Bush's higher-education record is, 'What record?' . . . By all accounts, Bush has avoided tackling controversial higher education issues."[6]

Isn't that what we need? A president with the courage to avoid tackling controversial issues?

Of course, race is always a controversial issue. So it is fair to ask why W, who never misses a photo op with a minority child, who loves to lecture us about how he wants the American Dream "to touch every willing heart," who is forever repeating platitudes about the power of education, who had the largest surplus in Texas history, has been cited for "huge shortfalls in financial support . . . [for Texas'] two historically black institutions, Prairie View A&M University and Texas Southern University."[7]

Okay, So He Hasn't Done Squat in Austin. What Would He Do in Washington?

He'd wreak havoc.

Bush supports vouchers—a pernicious scheme that's premised on the idea that the way to help underfunded public schools is to take money away from them and send it to elite, private academies. This is truly an idea tailor-made for Bush. The theory is that the public schools, feeling the pressure from students threatening to leave for private schools, will rise to the competition, and reinvent themselves as shining examples of academic excellence. The elegant and eloquent Mary McGrory of the *Washington Post* has likened this to the theory that if you're having trouble in your marriage, you should have an affair; your spouse will be so inspired by the competition, he or she will reinvent themselves into Super-Spouse. (Okay, perhaps that's the wrong metaphor for an ardent Clinton defender like me to use. But you get the point.)

Vouchers are an especially cruel hoax to the poor. They cynically suggest impoverished kids in poor-performing public schools can "escape" to elite private academies. And we all know those elite private academies are just dying to accept the flood of lower-income students. You always see the coach of the prep school polo team recruiting in East St. Louis, don't you? And even if they were willing to take them, Bush's voucher plan has a yearly maximum of $1,500 per child.[8] Bush's elite private academy, Andover, charges slightly more than $1,500 a year. More like $24,500 a year. So if you were disciplined, and you saved your annual Bush voucher, you could afford one year at Bush's elite private academy—in a little over sixteen years. And that doesn't include feed for the polo ponies.

The Bottom Line

Let's face it: Millie the Bush family dog has written more books than W has read. His talk about education is just that: talk.

Ninety percent of our kids go to public schools. And most of our public schools are very good. But some are failing. Here's what the two candidates' plans would do about it:

- Al Gore supports repairing 5,000 crumbling school buildings; Bush opposes it.

- Gore supports 100,000 new teachers; Bush opposes it.

- Gore supports universal prekindergarten; Bush opposes it.

- Gore has a plan to expand access to higher education so that every young person who wants to go to college can; Bush does not.

- Gore supports testing all new teachers; Bush does not.

- Gore's plan will identify and remove bad teachers; Bush's does not.

- Gore's plan calls for states to ensure that all teachers are qualified by 2004; Bush's does not.

Why doesn't Bush have proposals on any of these educational issues? Because he supports vouchers. It's kind of the "Let them eat cake" approach. (That's a historical allusion to Marie Antoinette, Governor. Karl Rove will explain it to you.)

Here's the real Bush plan for kids in failing schools—based on his own Horatio Alger story. (It's a literary allusion, Governor. Karl Rove will explain it to you.)

1. Get a trust fund;

2. Get admitted into the finest schools in America (you don't even have to go to class or study!);

3. Run for president on a platform of education reform, hiding your real agenda of abandoning public schools.

chapter 5

"It's Still the Economy ... and Bush Is Stupid!"

"We ought to make the pie higher."

(South Carolina Republican debate, 2/15/00)

"It's clearly a budget. It's got a lot of numbers in it."

(Reuters, 5/5/00)

When the last President George Bush got on *Air Force One* to fly to Houston and begin life as former President George Bush, unemployment was 7.1 percent; today it's around 4 percent. The poverty rate was 15.1 percent; today it's 12.7 percent. The Dow Jones Industrial Average was 3,242; today it's hovering around 11,000. Median family income (in constant 1998 dollars) was $33,839; today it's $38,885.[1]

The federal deficit was a record $290 billion a year; today we have a record projected surplus of $211 billion.[2] The national debt had climbed from just $1 trillion (accumulated under Presidents George Washington through Jimmy Carter) to $4 trillion (quadrupling under the twelve years of Presidents Reagan and Bush); today we're on a trajectory to completely eliminate the entire national debt in twelve years. Bill Clinton and Al Gore promised to create 8 million jobs; under their leadership we've created 22 million and counting. Home ownership rates are at an all-time high; minority unemployment rates at an all-time low.[3]

Now you, as a mere citizen, might look at that economic performance and think: Maybe we're heading in the right direction. Oh, but you, dear reader, are not possessed of the uncanny intellect and keen insight of George W. Bush. He can see behind the facade of the numbers and conclude that we should reverse course.

He calls for "Prosperity with a Purpose." But what's his purpose, you ask? To make the rich even richer, and keep the rest of us in our place.

George W. Bush's economic plan is a return to the trickle-down days of the 1980s. He wants to cut taxes for the rich, gut the social safety net, turn more and more power over to giant corporations, and limit the rights of working people. W is so 1980s he even had KC and the Sunshine Band play at his big Washington fund-raiser. You half expect to see him with his hair slicked back à la Gordon Gekko (the Michael Douglas character in *Wall Street*) bellowing, "Greed is good!"

You're reading this, and you're thinking: Didn't we try this before? And didn't all that trickle down result in a few rich folks and corporations getting the gold mine while the rest of us got the shaft? Didn't those Reagan-Bush economic policies run up the debt, cripple our competitiveness, and drive us into a recession?

But here again, you lack the raw (if unappreciated) genius of George W. Bush. He's thinking, Maybe if we try it again it'll work the second time. Kind of like someone in a lifeboat from the *Titanic* saying, "Gee, I hope we hit another iceberg."

My friend and former boss, Bill Clinton, likes to say that the definition of insanity is "doing the same thing over and over again and expecting a different result."

But I'll give this to Bush: he's hell-bent on giving Trickle Down II (or, as Poppy might call it, "Voodoo Re-Do") a try.

Tax Cuts for the Rich: Now *There's* a Novel Idea

"It is not Reaganesque to support a tax plan that is Clinton in nature."

(Los Angeles, 2/23/00)

The centerpiece of the Bush economic plan is a ten-year $1.9 trillion tax cut that primarily benefits the rich. Now $1.9 trillion is, as we say in Texas, "a right smart o' money." But I guess it takes a lot of money to impress Bush's billionaire buddies. Because that's who stands to benefit the most from the Bush tax plan. The nonpartisan Citizens for Tax Justice found that under Bush's plan, the richest 10 percent get 60 percent of the benefits and the top 1 percent get nearly half (43 percent to be precise) of the entire Bush tax cut. The other 99 percent of us get to split the other half. That lucky 1 percent of taxpayers get a hefty $46,000 per year tax cut, while most average working families would get only $227—about 60 cents a day.[4]

Wow. Sixty cents a day. That's not even enough to buy a Coke in most vending machines. But it could be the most expensive 60 cents you ever received, because the total size of the Bush tax cut will make it impossible to pay off the national debt, might bring us back to the days of budget deficits, will make saving Social Security and Medicare infinitely more difficult—and forget about making any meaningful investments in our schools, our roads and bridges, our children's health, or in toxic cleanup. All that opportunity squandered, just so the richest 1 percent can suck up another $46,000 a year. Oh, and don't forget that big ol' 60 cents Junior is leaving on the table for you.

If it's all the same to you, W, you can take your 60 cents and stick it in your ear.

And remember: 60 cents a day is the number if you're an average working family. What about the working poor? What about the folks who need a little relief more than anyone else? The folks who mop floors and make beds and pick vegetables—all to stay off welfare; all to give their kids a better life. Well, Santa Bush has a little present for all his little peasants: $42 a year. Eleven cents a day. That's for you if you're in the bottom 20 percent of income—not the truly destitute, mind you, just working folks on the lower rungs of the pay ladder—you get 11 cents a day. Don't spend it all in one place.[5]

So let's do the math. If you're in the top 1 percent, you get 100 times more from Bush than if you're in the middle class, and 1,000 times more than if you're struggling to make ends meet. A hundred to one—or a thousand to one—is a sucker's bet. And that's what Bush is betting on: that you'll be a sucker and support him so he can repay his rich friends with a massive tax cut.

Right-wingers love to look at the surplus and ask, "Whose money is it?" Well, folks, it's your money. So don't let Bush give it to the rich.

Yes, it's your money. It's also your debt. And if Bush has his way it—that debt—is going to go way up. According to the Congressional Budget Office the entire non–Social Security, non-Medicare surplus (which is the real surplus available) is about $1.8 trillion.[6] And remember, the Republicans run the Congress, so by using the budget office's numbers we're using the Republicans' numbers. Bush looks at that $1.8 trillion and says, "Hey, I have a neat idea. Let's cut taxes on the rich by $1.9 trillion." But isn't a $1.9 trillion tax cut *more than* the entire $1.8 trillion surplus? you ask. Maybe to you. But for W, unburdened as he is by even simple mathematics, it's a great deal.

But maybe the math really does work if you're Bush. They say that charity begins at home. Especially in the George W. Bush home. Bush himself would save a pile from his own tax-cut plan. In fact, if it had been in effect in 1998, the year Bush made $15 million in income, Bush's tax cut would have saved him an estimated $877,125.[7]

A Red River of Ink in Texas?

How can I be so sure Bush would squander the surplus as president? 'Cause that's exactly what he's done as governor. At the beginning of 1999, George W. Bush had the largest budget surplus in Texas history: $6.4 billion. But he also had a burning ambition to show the wealthy windbags who run the Republican party that he was the man who could deliver them the tax cuts their greedy little Republican hearts desired. (And don't forget the Golden Rule of the Republican party: He Who Has the Gold, Rules.)

So Bush rammed through a massive $1.6 billion tax cut. When concerns were raised about whether the state could afford such a huge tax cut at the same time the cost of Medicaid, prisons, and other vital needs were rising, Bush's fellow Republican, the comptroller of public accounts, increased her budget estimate by $807 million in the closing weeks of the legislative session.[8] The tax cut passed, and Bush got the hell out of Dodge—to campaign for president on his shiny new tax cut.

Then, in January of 2000, warning signs began to appear. The Texas Department of Health's chief budget officer sent Bush a memo warning about a potential budget shortfall. Bush's office called it "Nothing to worry about." Said it was "very, very preliminary."[9] Bush was half right. It was very, very preliminary. But it was something to worry about. But rather than take care of the fiscal mess he'd created, Bush had to deal with the political mess he was in. John McCain was busy opening up a can of whup-ass on W up in New Hampshire, so Bush was hardly in a mood to deal with something as unimportant as whether he'd blown the budget back home.

But by midsummer of this year, however, there was no denying it. Texas was in a full-blown fiscal mess. Bush had taken the largest surplus in Texas history and squandered it. Nearly 90 percent of that $6.4 billion budget surplus is now gone, leaving only about $650 million standing between the Lone Star State and a budget deficit—the first time in nine years that Texas has faced a budget pinch.[10] How did it happen? State Representative Garnet Coleman, who sits on the budget-writing committee, says it was a matter of Bush's priorities, and Bush's tax cut came first. "The question is, did we budget enough money to meet all our needs? No, we did not," Coleman said. "Once something is set as a priority, it takes over other priorities."[11]

And for Bush, the priority then—and in the future—is "Damn the deficits! Cut taxes for the rich!"

Why Would a Guy Who Stands to Inherit a Fortune Support Repealing the Estate Tax? Is That a Trick Question?

In his shameless quest to toady to the idle rich, Bush has proposed repealing the one and only tax that is paid solely and exclusively by millionaires—and only on income they did nothing to earn, on wealth they did nothing to generate. The estate tax is only charged to the wealthiest 1.4 percent of all estates. So 98.6 percent of us don't have to worry about that dreaded combination of death and taxes. And in fact, two thirds of the revenue from the estate tax comes from just 0.2 percent of estates.[12] They are, by definition, the filthy rich. And besides that, they are dead. They don't need it. They won't miss it. As Don Henley sang, "They don't make hearses with luggage racks." The Pearly Gates is not, I'm told, the kind of place you can get a good table at just by greasin' St. Pete's hand with a couple of Ben Franklins.

Bush wants to abolish the millionaire's inheritance tax entirely. He and his billionaire buddies like to feed us a line of jive about how they want to repeal the estate tax so that family farms can be passed down from generation to generation. But we've had the estate tax since 1916, and farms have been handed down for eighty-four years under it. In fact, 95 percent of farms aren't covered by the estate tax, since you don't pay the first dime of tax until the estate is worth upward of $1.3 million per couple—and it's due to go up to $2 million per couple in a few years. Truth be told, only 0.5 percent of it the federal government collects comes from farm families.[13] 99.5 percent comes from non–farm millionaires.

So when Bush and his buddies start whining about how the estate tax hurts family farms, you can tell him, "That's déjà moo. I've heard that bull before."

It takes a lot of gall for a guy who may one day inherit a family fortune to be campaigning for the repeal of the estate tax. But our boy W has always made up in brass what he's lacked in brains.

Corporate Power Wins Big in Texas; Little Guys Lose Again

One issue Bush loves to talk about is his commitment to limit consumer lawsuits, which he views as a hindrance to a healthy bidness climate. As governor he signed legislation to limit damages to $200,000, made it harder for juries to punish corporations through punitive damages, made it tougher to sue for medical malpractice, and limited corporations' liability for deceptive trade practices.[14]

And maybe, just maybe, Bush's passion for protecting corporate power has something to do with the $5.6 million Bush has received in campaign donations from special interests who want to preserve their strength and limit your rights.[15] Companies like Philip Morris, Exxon, Mobil, Shell, and Dow all pushed for limits on citizen lawsuits in Texas. And their boy Bush sure delivered.[16]

"Business groups flocked to us," said Bush's chief strategist Karl Rove.[17] I'll bet they did, Karl. Vultures often flock to an easy meal they can pick clean.

Have any of these limitations on Texans' ability to defend themselves against powerful corporations in a court of law created a single job? Have they strengthened the Texas economy? Naaah. But that was never really the design. This is about protecting corporate power and restricting the rights of those pesky citizens who would dare to stand up to Corporate America. In fact, despite mandatory rate rollbacks written into the law by Democratic legislators, insurance companies in Texas have actually raised their rates and made windfall profits because of the drop in claims forced by the limits on lawsuits. During the three years after Bush's tort "reform" passed, auto insurance companies alone netted an unprecedented $3 billion, according to D. J. Powers, former general counsel for the Texas Department of Insurance. "I know the governor needs a plank in his campaign saying he saved money through tort reform, but it hasn't happened," says Birny Birnbaum, former chief economist for the Texas Insurance Department, who helped draft the rate rollback provision. "Consumers haven't been benefiting. The insurance companies have. They've raked in billions of dollars in excess profits since the reforms were passed."[18]

As governor, Bush has been great for powerful corporations, but lousy for people. "Once again Governor Bush stood up for the large corporations and against the average citizens of Texas," said Tom Smith, the Texas director of the reform group Public Citizen. "His policies have made it much more difficult for Texans to sue and recover when they're injured or to use punitive damages to get defective products off the market." [19]

Where's the Beef?

"Will the highways on the Internet become more few?"

(Concord, New Hampshire, 1/29/00)

Beyond cutting taxes for the rich, and sucking up to the powerful, the Bush economic plan is mighty thin. He pledges to continue the Clinton-Gore policies of free trade and strong federal research and development funding. He tries to pander to the high-tech sector by promising them (surprise!) tax cuts and an increase in the number of foreign workers who can come to America for high-tech jobs—an issue that's bound to ruffle some feathers among American working people who would be all too happy to take those high-tech tech jobs, if only W would support the training and skills they need to take them.

The Bottom Line

Bush likes to tell us he's a man of his word. And that's what scares me. He certainly kept his word to his rich supporters in Texas, handing them a tax cut that was skewed to the rich and squandered nearly all of the largest surplus in Texas history. And he certainly kept his word to the big corporations, the tobacco companies, and the insurance conglomerates in Texas. But if we make him president, he may not keep his word to you and me—we're expendable, after all. Look at all his promises and tell me they add up. He has pledged to:

1. Cut taxes by $1.9 trillion (mostly for the rich);

2. Return to Reagan-era levels of Pentagon spending;

3. Maintain or increase Clinton-era levels of education spending;

4. Partially privatize Social Security (a move even his supporters say will cost an additional $1 trillion);

5. And still balance the budget and reduce the national debt.

Folks, that's not just pie in the sky. That's a whole floating bakery.

And when push comes to shove, which promises do you think he'll break? The promises he's made to his wealthy supporters, or the promises he's made to us? Look at what happened in Texas. The oil companies got their tax cut. But what about the rest of us? We were promised tax relief, too. *Bzzzzzz.* Sorry. Thanks for playing. Turns out that most of the folks who were promised a property tax cut from Bush in 1997 didn't get one. The *Dallas Morning News* analyzed 1,036 school districts statewide and found that taxpayer savings "didn't materialize" with Bush's property tax legislation: "Most districts increased tax rates." Even Bush's loyal second-in-command, Republican lieutenant governor Rick Perry, called the 1997 Bush property tax cuts "Rather illusory. That tax cut didn't stand the test of time as well as many of us would have liked for it to," Perry said.[20]

I am not a cynic, but I'd bet heavy that even if he has to break his word to chumps like you and me, good ol' George will keep his word to pass monster tax cuts for the big-money boys who are bankrolling him—and who want to see a healthy return on their investment.

After all, it's just bidness.

chapter 6

Praise the Lord and Pass the Ammunition!

"If we win, we'll have a President . . . where we work out of their office. Unbelievably friendly relations."

> (National Rifle Association vice president Kayne Robinson, salivating over the NRA running the country if Bush becomes president, *Washington Post*, 5/4/00)

I am a hunter and a gun owner. In fact I own three guns, and I may be the first person to hang a stuffed deer head in the White House since Teddy Roosevelt. I am not, as Don Imus would say, some panty-sniffin', leg-warmer-loving wussie who wants to confiscate guns from law-abiding citizens. Along with my brother and my dad, I go hunting several times a year.

But even by my standards, George W. Bush is nuts.

No, he's worse than nuts. He's a suck-up, a toady, a butler, a servant, a lackey, a butt-boy (another Imus-ism) for the NRA. Look at his record:

Bush Supports Guns in Church

I'm not making this up. But in order for you to understand how Bush could sign a law allowing guns in church, let me give you some background on just how completely captive of the gun nuts Bush truly is.

In 1995, one of the first bills new Governor Bush signed reflected his true priorities. It was not an education bill or a health care bill or a child care bill. It was a gun bill. Bush repealed Texas' 125-year-old ban on carrying a concealed weapon. The Texas Police Chiefs Association lobbied against the bill, but the police were outgunned politically by the NRA. "Texas will be a better place because of this law," Bush said upon signing it. In order to pack heat in Texas, all you have to do is pass a background check, and complete ten entire hours of training.[1] By contrast, you need 150 hours of training before you can legally cut hair in Texas.[2]

I guess Governor Bush trusts his fellow Texans with a .45 that can blow you away more than he trusts them with a blow-dryer.

We Texans generally don't trust outsiders, but W seems to have taken a liking to them—perhaps because he's really from Connecticut. Bush signed a bill that allows non-Texans to carry a concealed weapon if they have a permit from their home state—even if they haven't attended that stringent, exhaustive, ten-hour training program.[3]

When Bush signed the law, the police and other assorted weenies predicted mayhem. Well, maybe they were right. In just the first few years under the Bush concealed weapons bill, 3,051 Texans with concealed weapons permits were arrested, including 27 for attempted murder and manslaughter. And it got worse over time. Felony and misdemeanor charges against concealed weapons permit holders increased 54 percent from the first year to the second year of the program.[4]

Okay, so after allowing folks to pack heat as they walk down the street—something they hadn't been able to do since the days of Judge Roy Bean and the Wild West—you would think Bush would look at the thousands of people with concealed weapons permits whom his police officers had to arrest, and come to the conclusion that the police were right and the gun nuts were wrong; that this was too dangerous to our police officers, and too foolish for our citizens.

But you would be wrong.

Instead, Bush decided that what Texas needed was more guns. Including in church. You see, the 1995 concealed weapons bill specifically exempted certain places from the right to carry—churches, synagogues, and other places of worship, hospitals, nursing homes, and amusement parks. It wasn't a very long list, but it must have annoyed the gun nuts to be barred from packing heat at Queen of Peace church or Astroworld amusement park. So the kooks came up with a bill to specifically allow Texans to carry guns in those banned places.

Once again, those pantywaist police officer chiefs opposed it. (When will they get some guts?) And this time they were joined by the Texas Municipal League, which represents 1,020 cities, and the Texas Catholic Conference.

They lost.

And Bush, ever the faithful toady to the gun nuts, signed it. So now, thanks to George W. Bush, my fellow Texans can bring their guns into church ("Praise the Lord and pass the ammunition!") and amusement parks (which should make the air-gun shooting galleries a whole lot more interesting).

The only way a church or other institution can now legally keep guns out is to post a sign as mandated by law. Get this:

1. The sign must say (word for word): "Pursuant to Section 30.06, Penal Code (trespass by holder of license to carry a concealed handgun), a person licensed under Article 4413(29ee), Revised Statues (concealed handgun law), may not enter this property with a concealed handgun." A sign that says "No Guns Allowed" will not do.

2. The sign must be in English and Spanish.

3. The sign must appear "in contrasting colors with block letters at least one inch in height."

4. The sign must be "displayed in a manner clearly visible to the public."[5]

There now, isn't that simple? All you need is a lawyer to figure out the precise wording, then a sign maker to ensure the size and colors are right. Then you need someone fluent in Spanish to translate it for you—and you're home free. (Or should I say gun-free?)

The folks at Six Flags amusement parks are not amused. And they're not stopping with just a sign. They've installed metal detectors to keep guns out of their parks. "We installed them as a direct response to the weapons law," said Nancy St. Pierre, a Six Flags spokesperson. "As a way to make sure our park remains a safe place for our visitors."[6] Spoilsports. (But if Dick Cheney had his way, we could defeat those metal detectors with plastic handguns. See "Cheney Mania! Poppy's Pick.")

Maybe the whole thing will work out. Maybe the churches were wrong. It would sure boost donations if the guy passing the collection plate in one hand was holding a .38 in the other. And young people would be a lot more attentive when visiting Gramps in the nursing home if they thought he might blow them away for being disrespectful.

I can laugh about this because I no longer live in Texas. But I still live in America. And if Bush were to become president, you can bet your blunderbuss he'll do everything the NRA wants—just as he's done in Austin.

Too Little, Too Late on the Gun Show Loophole

One look at his campaign promises and positions and you know it's true. Bush refused to support a mandatory background check for gun show purchases. But then he abruptly switched and announced his support for closing the gun show loophole—shortly *after* the Columbine High School shootings in Littleton, Colorado—and just hours after the Texas Legislature had killed a bill mandating such background checks. I guess timing is everything. When State Representative Debra Danberg, the House sponsor of the background check bill, was asked if the governor had made any effort to help her pass the legislation, she laughed. She said she only learned of Bush's alleged support after the bill had already been killed.[7]

And when the fight moved to Washington, Bush was once again back on the side of the NRA. He opposed the Lautenberg Amendment in the Senate, which would have required background checks at gun shows.[8] It passed the Senate only because a courageous vice president was willing to cast the tie-breaking vote, while Bush cowered with the gun lobby.[9]

Bush also backed NRA-supported legislation in the House of Representatives that would have weakened our existing gun laws by making it more difficult to conduct background checks at gun shows. The FBI estimated that 17,000 criminals who were denied guns under the current law would have been able to obtain them if the NRA-backed bill had become law.[10]

A Flip-Flop on Trigger Locks

When he was asked, in 1999, if he was a supporter of mandatory child safety locks on all guns, Bush said, "No, I'm not. I'm for voluntary safety locks on guns."[11] In February 2000 Bush was attacking John McCain in the South Carolina primary for supporting mandatory trigger locks.[12] But one month later, Bush said he would not push for trigger lock legislation, but he would sign it if it passed.[13] I guess necessity is the mother of invention.

Special Rights for Gun Manufacturers

Bush supported and signed legislation that was branded "the gun lobby's top priority"—giving gun makers special protection from being held legally liable for the design and marketing of their products.[14] The bill also banned cities from suing gun makers—even though not a single city in Texas had filed such a suit.[15]

It's amazing that a guy who has such faith in juries that he trusts them to take a human life (or hundreds of them in his case) can at the same time so distrust juries that he won't even let them hear a case against a gun manufacturer.

Bush Doesn't Even Enforce the Laws That Are on the Books

One of the favorite lines of NRA suck-ups like Bush is to claim that we don't need new laws, we just need to enforce the laws that are already on the books. You're right on that one, Governor. Under Bush's watch, Texas law enforcement authorities were aware of hundreds of convicted felons who may have illegally possessed firearms, but did nothing about it. Federal law prohibits convicted felons from possessing guns. Yet hundreds of convicted felons have shown up—gun in hand—to attend the required training course. More than 600 applicants for a concealed weapons permit have been turned down because they were felons. As of December 1999 (the latest date for which I could get statistics) not one of them had been prosecuted.[16]

The Bottom Line

The bottom line on Bush and guns is scary. Guns in church, guns on the street, and in nursing homes and amusement parks. Hundreds of armed felons going unprosecuted. And the NRA setting up shop in the Oval Office. My friends on the right love to snicker and sneer about the embarrassing and sinful things President Clinton did in and around the Oval Office. But what Bush and the NRA are planning to do there may be even worse.

chapter 7

To Die For: Bush and the Environment

"There's no such thing as being too closely aligned to the oil business in West Texas."

(*Lubbock Avalanche Journal*, 3/30/78)

"Bush represents the biggest threat to the environment of any leading major party presidential candidate."

(Deb Callahan, president, League of Conservation Voters, 1/13/00)

"We believe the air crisis is due to the intentional acts and conscious indifference of Governor Bush."

(Meg Haenn of the Texas Air Crisis Campaign,
a coalition of forty-four environmental groups,
Dallas Morning News, 10/20/99)

Like me, George W. Bush is a hunter and a fisherman. Unlike me, George W. Bush is also a total suck-up to corporate polluters.

Guess which impulse W sides with when the two collide?

You're getting good at this. At every critical juncture as governor of Texas, Bush has sided with the big-money corporate polluters and against the environment. Of course, the big-money polluters have also sided with Bush. That makes him kind of a happy hooker on the environment.

You don't have to wear Birkenstocks and sing Raffi songs to be an environmentalist. Most hunters and fishermen are what's known as "hook and bullet environmentalists." We know that wilderness, clean water, clean air, and curbs on urban sprawl are essential to wildlife habitat, and thus to our sports. That's why most hunters and fishermen are strongly committed to a clean environment. And most parents know that every time they get their children a drink of water from the tap, they're pouring into their children whatever Corporate America has poured into the water supply. Parents in cities with high rates of childhood asthma, caused by toxic emissions in the air—they're environmentalists, too. We may differ stylistically from our tree-hugger friends, but the result is the same.

Whether you care about hunting and fishing, drinking the water, or breathing the air, you should know this: George W. Bush has been a one-man wrecking crew on the environment. On clean water, his attitude is "Let them drink Perrier." Clean air? Let them buy a ranch out far away from the city. That's what Bush did.

"Please Don't Pollute": Bush Let His Contributors Design "Voluntary" Pollution Controls

Some of the biggest sources of air pollution in Texas are what are known as "grandfathered companies." Now "grandfather" has a kindly, gentle connotation, but in this context it's better to think of them as dirty old men. "Grandfathered companies" are companies whose plants were under construction or already up and running—and belching fumes— when the 1971 Clean Air Act was passed. Thirty-six percent of industrial air pollution in Texas comes from these dirty old men.[1]

Here's how Bush dealt with the dirty old men: he *asked them not to pollute*. Pretty please. With sugar on top. I'm not kidding. In 1997, Bush pushed a *voluntary* permits plan for the dirty old men. Voluntary! Texas didn't have voluntary rules on speeding when I was collecting tickets on I-35. Why the hell should corporate polluters be expected to voluntarily comply with emissions controls?

Because to W, they're not just corporate polluters. They're contributors. Bush allowed grandfathered-company representatives who had contributed to his campaign to help draft the Bush environmental plan.

From 1994 to 1999, Bush took $1,371,795 in gubernatorial and presidential campaign contributions from grandfathered companies' PACs and company officials. Why not just eliminate the middleman and let the corporate polluters run the state? Now do you see why I call Bush a happy hooker?

Of the 984,000 tons of air pollution produced by grandfathered companies, 741,000 tons—75 percent—came from companies that have donated $500 or more to Bush's gubernatorial races from 1994 to 1998. In 1999 Bush accepted at least $11,500 from a grandfathered company that had written in a 1997 letter sent to Bush's environmental policy director and to other dirty old men, "In early March, while discussing the National Ambient Air Quality Standards Issue with Governor Bush, he asked us to work with his office to develop the concepts of a voluntary program."[2]

But if Bush was cleaning up in terms of campaign contributions, his voluntary plan wasn't doing much to clean up the air. Though Bush claimed his voluntary plan was a success, one year after implementing the program less than one half of 1 percent of emissions from the grandfathered plants had been reduced. In 1999, only three of the thirty-six plants that had pledged to reduce emissions had actually done so.[3]

Now, do I have any proof that those contributions in any way affected Bush's decision-making process? No. But something stinks—and it's more than just the polluted air.

We're Number One! Houston Passes Los Angeles as Dirtiest City in America

I grew up in a little town not far from Houston. Houston is a great city, full of piss and vinegar. As any Houstonian will tell you, the first word spoken from the surface of the moon was "Houston." And yet, Houston has always had something of an inferiority complex. The Dallas Cowboys were always winning Super Bowls. The Houston Oilers never even went to the Super Bowl—until they moved to Al Gore's Nashville.

So Houston yearns for recognition. But not this kind. In 1999, Houston overtook Los Angeles as the city with the dirtiest air in America. Houston had the most violations of federal health ozone standards. It also had a higher number of peak days than Los Angeles. Ozone is really nasty stuff. It's a key component of smog, and a respiratory irritant. Breathing it is painful, dirty—and dangerous.[4] A 1999 study conducted by the city of Houston shows that Houston's air pollution may have caused at least 435 premature deaths and as many as 1,196 new cases of chronic bronchitis annually. Dirty air is also expensive. Houston has spent between $2.9 billion and $3.1 billion on health problems attributable to the city's ozone and airborne particles.[5] Hundreds of people dead before their time. Thousands sick with bronchitis. And billions spent to deal with it.

I hope the Bush campaign chokes on its dirty money.

If it seems like I'm getting personal to you, it's because this *is* personal to me. I have eight nieces and nephews (soon to be nine) growing up in Texas. Four of them (soon to be five!) in the Houston area. These babies have to breathe the crap and crud that Bush's contributors are spewing into the air. So when I see statistics about hundreds of people dying before their time, and thousands more fighting bronchitis for their next breath, they're not just statistics to me. They are potentially my nieces and nephews, my brothers and sisters-in-law; or my dad, retired and fishing in Galveston.

Of course, my family's kids aren't the only ones at risk. As a result of Bush's flawed plan, almost 230,000 Texas children in seven urban counties may be exposed to as much as 295,000 tons of air pollution each year because they attend schools within two miles of older industrial plants that are under Bush's voluntary permit program.[6]

And—who'd of thunk it?—it seems almost that none of the schools that are next to the filth-spewing factories are elite private academies. Can you imagine the coincidence? Stunning, isn't it? So once again, under the Compassionate Conservative, it's the poor who suffer most. A 1999 study found that 10 percent of the Hispanic and African-American children in Houston's inner cities suffer from asthma—twice the level previously measured just two years before. Asthma sufferers are especially threatened by increases in ozone levels, as those pollutants are known to irritate the condition and trigger attacks.[7]

It's not just asthma sufferers who are harmed by this. In 1999, ozone in Houston was so bad that Harris County judge Robert Eckels announced a new system to notify area schools when the smog levels made it dangerous for students to practice sports outside. On high smog days—let's call them "Bush Days"—athletes had experienced "coughing fits and other respiratory problems," according to the *Houston Chronicle*. It's outrageous. How would you feel if your son was a high school athlete getting sick just from breathing the air at football practice?

To give you an idea of just how bad it is, the national standard for ozone is 125 parts per billion; the highest reading in Deer Park, a blue-collar part of Houston, was 251 parts per billion in October 1999.[8]

And there's no doubt that Bush bears responsibility for this. A coalition of forty-four environmental groups called the Texas Air Crisis Campaign released a report in 1999 detailing how Texas air quality had deteriorated under Bush. "We believe the air crisis is due to the intentional acts and conscious indifference of Governor Bush, his appointees to the Texas Natural Resource Conservation Commission and the Legislature. There are both sins of omission and sins of emission," said Meg Haenn of the campaign. The group blamed Bush's poor vehicle emissions program and his allowing grandfathered companies to continue polluting with no mandatory regulations.[9]

And yet Bush just doesn't seem to care. Texas cities have repeatedly failed federal emissions standards since 1994, and Bush did little about the problem. A city is demoted in air pollution status by the federal government if it exceeds permissible ozone limits more than once a year from 1994 to 1996: Dallas, for example, exceeded them nine times in 1994, fifteen times in 1995, and four times in 1996. In 1999, Bush's environmental administrators claimed they did not have enough warning to get a clean air plan together.[10] Not enough warning? Didn't the twenty-eight violations in three years kinda give you a clue?

Don't Drink the Water Either

The Texas Center for Policy Studies took a look at water quality in Texas, and found that Bush has a slightly better record on water than he does on air pollution—but not much. "The overall water quality in

Texas' classified reservoirs has declined since 1992," according to the center's study. In addition, "a third of the state's rivers and streams probably violate federal water quality standards, though no one is certain because the state declines to test them all." [11]

To his credit, Bush did propose increased funds for evaluations of polluted streams, and other efforts, but his proposal failed to request the additional state employees necessary to carry out this work. The League of Conservation Voters said Bush didn't push his funding recommendations with the legislature, and as a result, while the legislature did pass some additional money for evaluation of polluted streams, the legislature did not approve the funding necessary for other critical water quality programs—a move that could lead to more lax enforcement and increased water pollution problems.[12]

The Watchdogs Are Lapdogs

There's that phrase again: "lax enforcement." Seems like that phrase keeps popping up whenever we look at Bush's record on the environment. Why has his enforcement of environmental laws been so lax? Because that's the way Bush wants it.

State Representative Lon Burnham of Fort Worth says, "State environmental officials appointed by Bush have been a disaster, and it started the month he took office. Bush has shown a total disregard for public health and an allegiance to private profit." [13] Now, Lon's a Democrat, and a former compadre of mine from Texas Democratic campaigns, so you might be a tad skeptical when he calls Bush's appointees "a disaster." So decide for yourself:

All of Bush's appointees to the Texas Natural Resource Conservation Commission (TNRCC, and pronounced "Train Wreck") had pro-industry, anti-regulation backgrounds. All of them. Every one of 'em.[14] And you know George. At Harvard Business School they taught him to delegate. So he puts the corporate bigwigs in charge of his environmental agency, and lets them do what they will. I don't blame them; I really don't. When someone puts a fox in charge of guarding the henhouse, you don't blame the fox.

As part of its continuing mission to cater to corporate polluters,

Bush's TNRCC has adopted a policy of giving companies up to two weeks' notice before routine inspections. "Who isn't going to look good when the inspector comes if you have this much advance notice?" asked Mary Kelly of the Texas Center for Policy Studies. A TNRCC memo issued in September 1995 states, "Ideally, this notification should occur one to two weeks prior to the inspection date." Officials at the commission say this is necessary to ensure company personnel are available when inspections are made.[15] It's also just good manners. And W is nothing if not well bred.

Under Bush, TNRCC has been especially troubled by allegations of environmental racism. At least nine civil rights complaints against the TNRCC were filed with the EPA from 1994 to 1999, more than against any other state environmental agency in the nation. The complaints charge that the TNRCC allows excess pollution in areas that are predominantly Hispanic, African-American, or poor. "The TNRCC's handling of [one of the cases] is another example that Governor George Bush Jr.'s environmental justice program at TNRCC is a complete sham," said Neil Carman, a former state air pollution official and the clean air director of the Texas chapter of the Sierra Club.[16]

When Pollution Levels Exceed the Limits, Just Raise the Limits

After Dallas violated the federal standard for ozone twenty-six times in one summer, Bush's TNRCC sprang into action. With alacrity, with dispatch, with a liveliness rarely seen in a bureaucracy, they proposed bold action to bring Big D's air in compliance with federal clean air standards.

They asked the EPA to lower the standards.

Kind of like in *This Is Spinal Tap* when the band insists their amplifier is louder because the knob goes to 11. One TNRCC commissioner asked the staff to come up with a scientific defense of the lower standard. "It seems that Texas is trying to clean up the air with statistics instead of pollution control. This is a bad idea," said Ron White, the director of environment for the radical lefty American Lung Association.[17]

Bush Donors Turned Superfund into "Corporate Welfare"

In their study "Superfund a Super Deal for Texas Polluters," Texas Public Employees for Environmental Responsibility (PEER) showed that industries that developed the Bush-supported plan to overhaul state Superfund laws had given Bush at least $3.5 million in his 1994 and 1998 gubernatorial campaigns. According to PEER, the relationship between industry campaign contributions and Bush shows "how industry was able to turn a Superfund program that was designed to clean up communities contaminated by toxic pollution into another corporate welfare program," and "these industries have long had clout in Texas state government, but it was not until George W. Bush was elected Governor that industry was able to get legislation signed to take the teeth out of the state Superfund law."[18]

The Bottom Line

Texas is, in highly biased opinion, the most beautiful state in America. It has sprawling forests, breathtaking canyons, hundreds of miles of rivers—and a governor who has allowed his corporate donors to trash it. Bush's willingness—eagerness—to allow polluters to make children sick just from breathing the air had better give you pause. Unless, of course, you don't plan on breathing if W becomes president.

chapter 8

Social Insecurity

"There's not going to be enough people in the system to take advantage of people like me."

> (On the coming Social Security crisis, Wilton, Connecticut, 6/9/00)

"Maybe, maybe not."

> (When asked if future Social Security recipients will get at least as much under his privatization plan as they would under the current system, *Dallas Morning News*, 5/15/00)

"I've never been a long-term planner about anything. I have lived my life with more of a short-term focus."

> (*Texas Monthly*, 5/94)

Republicans have always hated Social Security. And George W. Bush has always been a Republican. So I'm more than a tad skeptical when W talks about wanting to "fix" Social Security. Kind of reminds me of the vet who "fixed" my dog Gus. After the "fix," that which once worked just fine didn't work no more. And Gus was none too happy about the deal.

George W. Bush wants to neuter Social Security. His plan to cut taxes for the rich by $1.9 trillion, while risking a huge portion of the Social Security Trust Fund in the stock market, could spell the end of Social Security as we know it.

Think I'm being alarmist? I wish. Check out the *Houston Chronicle*:

"Bush on Tuesday said his plan to create private savings accounts could be the first step toward a complete privatization of Social Security."[1]

Complete privatization of Social Security. Haven't we tried that before? Oh, yeah, back in the Depression, before Roosevelt created Social Security. The retirement system was completely privatized then. You worked, then you retired, and if the money ran out, you were broke. Of course, even then the system wasn't completely private. There were county poor farms where the destitute could live and work—until they died. I wonder if that's too much government involvement for W?

To his credit, Bush is being honest about what he wants. He doesn't want to tinker with the system. No, he wants to take the single most successful government program of the twentieth century and reinvent it in his image.

I might feel better about the whole thing if he'd actually gone to class when he was enrolled in the Harvard Business School. But at least he's candid when he declares that his proposal to privatize about 16 percent of Social Security is just the beginning. More like the beginning of the end. As the *New York Times* reported: "Answering a question about his plan, Mr. Bush said that the government could not go 'from one regime to another overnight.' He said: 'It's going to take a while to transition to a system where personal savings accounts are the predominant part of the investment vehicle. And so, this is a step toward a completely different world and an important step.'"[2]

A completely different world. But what will Bush's brave new world look like? (That was an allusion to Aldous Huxley, Governor. Karl Rove will explain it to you.) Well, Bush admitted it was "conceivable" that a worker who opted for Bush's privatized scheme could wind up worse off than under the old, guaranteed Social Security system.[3] And he was even more blunt in the *Dallas Morning News:* "Asked whether he envisions a system in which future beneficiaries would receive no less than they would have under the current system, Mr. Bush said, 'Maybe, maybe not.'"[4]

Maybe, maybe not? Maybe, maybe not! That is not what seniors who want to retire in dignity and security want to hear, Governor.

Maybe, maybe not is an acceptable answer from the weatherman when you ask him if it's going to rain. But it's not an acceptable answer from your heart surgeon when you want to know if the new, transplanted heart is really going to be better than the old heart.

And it gets worse. As the *New York Times* reported: "Bush also refused to say how much benefits might be reduced for workers who created private investment accounts. 'That's all up for discussion,' Mr. Bush said."⁹

So this we know: There's no guarantee under Bush's plan that your benefits won't be cut. There's no guarantee that your investments won't go down. There's no guarantee that if they go down (say, if you invest in a company as poorly run as Bush's El Busto Oil Company) that the government will make you whole.

A Social Security system without guarantees is like a car without wheels. You can shine it up all you like, but it can't take you where you need to go.

One of the ways Bush hopes to build support for his system is to undermine confidence in the current system. His plan has no guarantees, so he pretends that the current system doesn't either, declaring, "First of all, there's no guarantees in Social Security today. . . . There are no guarantees."

Oh? Of course there are. The Full Faith and Credit of the United States of America stands behind the government-run, government-guaranteed Social Security benefits. Bush can't name a single time in seven decades when the government failed to deliver on that guarantee. He wants to pretend it isn't there now, since there truly are no guarantees in his plan.

And if the benefits are not guaranteed, the risks are. The stock market is inherently risky. That's why it often yields greater rewards. But Bush tries to hide the ugly reality that markets can go down. He simply refused to answer Sam Donaldson's question about what he would do for someone who lost their Social Security investment in the stock market. Look at this exchange:

DONALDSON: All I'm asking is whether you think the government should make good any losses for retirees from their accounts?

BUSH: There will be a lot of discussions about the particulars of the plans.

DONALDSON: Well, what do you think?

BUSH: But one of the things that's most important is to understand that giving younger workers the option to manage some of their money in safe vehicles is going to be a heck of a lot better rate of return on moneys invested than the current system.

DONALDSON: But, Governor, your opponent says it's not safe.

BUSH: You cannot justify the current—my opponent says a lot of things. But you can't justify the current system.

(CROSSTALK)

DONALDSON: But I want you to answer the question, sir. You're dodging the question.

BUSH: I'm not dodging the question.

DONALDSON: All right, I'll state the question again. Should the government guarantee against losses in Individual Retirement Accounts?

BUSH: But Sam, there are no guarantees today.

DONALDSON: So the answer is no?

BUSH: There are no guarantees in the system today. And if you think there are, then I would like for you to review the voting record of my opponent.[6]

Whew! I'll say this for Sam: he done his damnedest. But trying to get Bush to admit that his plan for Social Security has no real security is like trying to nail Jell-O to the wall. Of course, the good governor is full of beans when he says Al Gore's voting record proves there are no guarantees. What he's referring to was the 1993 Clinton-Gore economic package, which subjected a larger percentage of the Social Security income of the wealthiest retirees to taxation. That's all. And it only applied to folks whose net worth averaged around a million dollars. So, by Bush's logic, because Clinton and Gore raised taxes on the rich, Bush should have the right to cut Social Security for the poor.

And they say he's dumb.

Lots of serious people have weighed in on the notion of investing Social Security funds in the stock market, and it makes them nervous. Because, rumor has it, markets can go down. Now, I realize that hasn't happened since, well, since the last time we had a Bush in the White House. But seasoned veterans of Wall Street like Bob Rubin tell me it has happened. A report from the nonpartisan General Accounting Office noted, "Caution is warranted in counting on future stock returns in designing Social Security reform." The report goes on: "However, an average over nearly a century obscures the reality that stock returns fluctuate substantially from year to year. Over the past 70 years or so, stock returns were negative in nearly one out of four years. There is no guarantee that investing in the stock market, even over two or three decades, will yield the long-term average return."[7]

What if Bush is wrong? What if the markets go down? We could be heading for a government bailout that made the Reagan-Bush Savings & Loan bailout look like fixing a lemonade stand. A report done by Joseph J. Cordes and C. Eugene Steuerle for the Urban Institute said: "Privatization proposals that would allow individuals to 'keep' gains from private accounts in good times but require the government to maintain a floor in bad times would encourage individuals to take excessive risk. The consequences to the government would be similar to those when the savings and loan financial sector essentially went bankrupt."[8]

Now, to be fair to W (and I'm nothing if not fair to W) I should note that Bush has refused to say he will guarantee against losses in the stock market. And the Urban Institute study shows why. That's why Sam Donaldson had to chase him around the room so unsuccessfully. Bush doesn't want a system in which the rewards of risk taking are absorbed by the individual, but the risk is covered by the government. Or, rather, he doesn't want *you* to have such a deal. It was fine for him. He made $15 million on a stadium deal in which the taxpayers of Arlington, Texas, put up all the money to build him a stadium, but all the profit went to Bush and his partners. When the team was sold, Bush walked away with a cool $15 million. And the people of Arlington, who took the risk, got nothing.

This is classic Bush: he wants to abandon you to the vicissitudes of the market. He's happy to leave you in a sink-or-swim environment. But his butt has never been on the line. He's always had a sugar daddy— either big-money friends trying to suck up to Poppy, or the taxpayers of Arlington. (See "Bush as a Bidnessman.") Maybe that's why he's always smirking. He's playing us for suckers.

Would Bush Make Social Security Go "El Busto"?

Despite what you've heard from the Cassandras in the media (It's a mythological allusion, Governor. Karl Rove will explain it to you), Social Security is in fine shape. Even under the worst-case scenarios it's solvent until 2037. And that's if we do absolutely nothing to improve it. Al Gore's Social Security plan would pay off the national debt and still make Social Security solvent at least until the year 2050. Back in 1983, when we had a real Social Security crisis, the system was just months from insolvency. Today we are anywhere from thirty-seven to fifty years away from a problem, and Chicken Littles like George W. Bush are trying to tell you Social Security is collapsing.

Bull.

Even the dire predictions of insolvency in 2037 are based on economic assumptions that our economy will only grow at half the rate it's been growing for most of the past century. And if that's true, and economic growth slows by 50 percent, we're going to have a lot more immediate problems than Social Security becoming insolvent in thirty-seven years.

Bush wants you to believe Social Security is on the brink of disaster so you'll think his privatization plan is the only way out. In truth, his privatization plan would actually speed up the date of insolvency by as many as fourteen years, according to a study by the Center on Budget and Policy Priorities.[9]

The Plan with the Trillion-Dollar Hole

But let us, for argument's sake, assume that Bush is right; assume that investing one-sixth of the Social Security Trust Fund in the stock market is a terrific idea. There's still one little detail, which the economists call the transition costs. Moving our Social Security system from one based on government-guaranteed benefits to one of private risk and return will not be cheap.

Let's say you're living from paycheck to paycheck. The money comes in, the landlord gets paid. Then one day someone tells you that you've got to pay the whole year's rent in advance. That's what Bush's proposal is like. Right now, the little box on your paycheck marked "FICA" goes straight from your paycheck to your grandmother's Social Security check, not to some savings account in Washington with your name on it. Your payments go to current beneficiaries. And when you're a beneficiary, the payments of current workers will go to you. It's not really a savings account. It's an intergenerational transfer payment. (Now, I know we're getting too technical for W, but he's already given up reading by now, so let's keep having this grown-up conversation while he channel-surfs for reruns of *Animal House*.)

So, W comes in and says "Hold everything!" Under his plan you get to hold back 16 percent of the Social Security tax you're currently paying (and which currently goes straight to Grandma) and invest it in the stock market. Does Grandma suddenly lose 16 percent of her benefits? That hardly seems fair. But the money's got to come from somewhere, or else Grandma's going to end up eating Alpo.

And it ain't chump change. According to the Center for Budget and Policy Priorities, Bush's privatization plan would cost $900 billion over the first ten years. These costs occur because the Social Security system must simultaneously pay out current benefits, at the same time that privatization drains over 16 percent of the money coming into the system. Combine this with the cost of Bush's $1.9 trillion tax cut, and the Bush plan will leave multitrillion-dollar debts as far as the eye can see.[10]

How does Bush plan to deal with the trillion-dollar hole in his Social Security plan? Well, the Associated Press reports "Bush hasn't fully accounted for the costs of moving from the current system to his proposed one."[11] Needless to say, this little oversight does not sit well with seniors. Martin Corry, director of federal affairs for the American Association of Retired Persons, frets, "With a reduction in the payroll tax, that money has to be made up, or, unfortunately, it leads to difficult trade-offs."[12] (That's fancy talk for, "Open up the Alpo, Grandma!")

One Way for Bush to Plug the Hole in His Plan: Cut Benefits

Bush himself seems open to cutting benefits. As the *Wall Street Journal* reported: "Asked whether a reduction in guaranteed benefits is inevitable to make the shift to personal accounts affordable, Mr. Bush replied: 'That's what I call a transition cost.' "[13] You may call it a transition cost, Governor. The people whose benefits you're going to cut are going to have a few other words to describe it.

In an outburst of candor, Bush's chief economic adviser, Larry Lindsey, admitted that Bush's plan would "absolutely" cut benefits. Under Bush's plan, Lindsey said, "reductions in the guaranteed amounts of benefits that will go to plan participants are absolutely obvious. So I will say it." According to *Newsweek*, "Bush doesn't exactly stress [Lindsey's statement]. Or the fact that if you pick the investment option and do badly, your combined stock and guaranteed benefit would be less than the regular Social Security package."[14]

As my kids would say, "Duh."

Another Way for Bush to Plug the Hole in His Plan: Raise the Retirement Age

One way he might deal with the huge cost is to raise the retirement age. Bush admitted as much on *Meet the Press*. When Tim Russert asked him, "Would you look at raising the eligibility age for the boomer generation?" Bush replied, "Yeah . . . as part of a trade-off or as part of an opportunity for the boomers and the preboomer-boomers to be able to manage their own accounts."[15]

Great. Raising the retirement age to seventy or seventy-five may be fine for the trust-funded offspring of the Eastern elite aristocracy. It may not be a problem for people (and I'm not naming names here) who've never worked a day in their life; folks who have cruised through life on their Poppy's name and their family's connections and their cronies' money. But what about a waitress, who carries heavy trays every day? Bush wants her to work till she drops? What about farmworkers who stoop and sweat in the sun so yuppie swine like W can have garden-fresh salads at the country club? What about cops who get shot at, or firefighters who breathe toxic fumes, or garbagemen who lift hundreds of heavy garbage cans every day?

Bush's Plan Would Be Especially Rough on African-Americans, Women, and Working Families (What a Surprise!)

Of course, Bush's entire plan would be harder on African-Americans than white folks, since nearly 80 percent of African-American seniors depend entirely on Social Security for their retirement income. (The figure is about 60 percent for white seniors.) Since they're more dependent on Social Security, African-Americans would be more exposed to the risks of stock market fluctuations.[16]

Women would be similarly threatened, since women are more likely to rely on Social Security for their primary source of retirement benefits. And it's not just lefty liberals who have sounded the alarm about how women will be hurt by privatization. John Mueller is the senior vice president and chief economist of Lehrman Bell Mueller Cannon, Inc., and a former adviser to former Bush cabinet member and Bob Dole running mate Jack Kemp. He testified before the House Social Security Subcommittee that "the largest group of losers from 'privatizing' Social Security would be women. This is true for women in all birth-years, all kinds of marital status, all kinds of labor-market behavior, and all income levels." Mueller came to that conclusion after conducting a comprehensive study on Social Security privatization for the Center for the Preservation of Social Security and Medicare.[17]

Here, as a public service, is George W. Bush's *real* plan for Social Security:

Plan A:

1. Invest in the market (ask Poppy's brother and other Wall Street insiders for hot tips);

2. If your investment tanks, get bailed out by big-money boys. (This works better if you are wise enough to choose a father who

is president of the United States; if you haven't had the foresight
to have such a Poppy, see Plan B.)

Plan B:

1. Invest in the market;

2. If your investment tanks, develop a taste for Alpo.

What Do the Experts Say?

By now, your head is likely spinning. And while I care deeply about Social Security, and spent a great deal of time studying it when I was a
senior aide to the president, I don't pretend to be an expert. But here's
what a bunch of smart folks who have looked at Bush's plan have to say
about it:

- *Without the details, the Bush plan looks like its "numbers don't
  add up."* The Center on Budget and Policy Priorities' Robert
  Greenstein said that "In the absence of any more detail, it simply looks like the numbers don't add up until he provides more
  detail on how could he finance a plan like this." [18]

- *Bush could "fundamentally alter" Social Security "without
  guaranteeing its financial security."* The *Washington Post* says
  that if Bush's economic assumptions are wrong—which several
  economists seem to think they will be—"he would fundamentally alter the character of the highly popular program without
  guaranteeing its financial security." The *Post* added that "Several analysts are skeptical that the stock market will do as well
  in the future as Bush suggests." [19]

- *Even Bush's adviser acknowledged the Bush plan will deplete the
  trust fund.* Bush's chief economic adviser, Larry Lindsey, acknowledged that Bush's Social Security plan would deplete the
  cash surplus in a few years. Lindsey said that the Treasury Department would then have to make good on Social Security
  bonds. Moreover, Lindsey acknowledged, the government may
  need to dip into general revenues—i.e., rely on budget surpluses—to cover the cost of transitioning to private accounts in
  2030. [20]

The Bottom Line

If we adopt Al Gore's plan, you can invest in the stock market to your heart's content, without risking your guaranteed benefits (that's why his plan is called "Retirement Savings Plus"), and the Social Security system will be in the black until 2050. If we do nothing, you'll still have your guaranteed Social Security benefits, and the system will be solvent until 2037. But if we adopt the Bush plan, your guaranteed benefits will be cut, the retirement age might be raised, there's no guarantee that your stock market investments will make up for the cuts, and the system will go broke in 2023.

What a deal.

chapter 9

Why Help Working Families When You Can Suck Up to Wealthy Families?

"I know how hard it is for you to put food on your families."
> (Greater Nashua, New Hampshire, Chamber of Commerce,
> 1/27/00)

"I think we need not only to eliminate the tollbooth to the middle class, I think we should knock down the tollbooth."
> (Nashua, New Hampshire, *New York Times*, 2/1/00)

Perhaps because he's never held an honest job—that is to say a job he didn't get because of his family's name or his father's contacts—George W. Bush has a remarkably consistent record of opposing anything and everything that could help working people. His attitude seems to be: I made a fortune with nothing but a trust fund and a father in the White House. Why can't you?

On issues of working families, Bush promises a return not just to the 1980s, when Ronald Reagan told us ketchup was a vegetable, but all the way back to the 1930s. His positions today are virtually indistinguishable from Herbert Hoover's. Think about this:

Bush Opposes a National Minimum Wage

Trying to have it both ways, Bush says he supports an increase in the federal minimum wage, but only if states could opt out, "a condition that could render a proposed increase meaningless," according to the Associated Press.[1] This country has had a national minimum wage since the 1930s. But by allowing states to opt out, Bush would gut the minimum wage. States would be forced into a "race to the bottom," in which they would first opt out of the national minimum wage, then reduce their state-based minimum wage in order to attract businesses. The pressure to cut the minimum wage would be tremendous. If states had the power to ignore the national minimum wage, there would be no such thing as a minimum wage in this country—exactly what Bush's powerful corporate supporters want.

"Oh, Begala," you may be thinking, "Bush seems like such a nice guy, I'll bet he'd support a strong minimum wage in his state." One word: wrong. Texas does have a minimum wage, of $3.35 an hour. Six bills to increase the Texas minimum wage have been introduced since Bush took office.[2] He didn't support any of them (in fact he actively opposed raising the state minimum wage),[3] and none of them passed.

Refusing to raise the state's minimum wage matters. Here's why: Texas workers employed in the service sector—agriculture and domestic services—are covered by Texas' state minimum wage of $3.35 an hour. That means if you bust your butt picking onions in the Rio Grande Valley, or scrubbing floors in Houston, or cleaning toilets for rich people in Bush's tony neighborhood in Dallas, and you work full time, forty hours a week, all year 'round, you take home the princely sum of—are you ready for this?—$6,700 per year.[4] Now, if those folks were smart, and set aside fifteen years' salary, they could be one of Bush's $100,000 donors, and Bush would meet with them, pose for a photo, and do their bidding, just as he does for the fat cats who fund his campaign. Why should W be punished for the lack of foresight, the lack of savings, the lack of civic involvement of these people? If they'd just play the game according to Bush's rules, I'm sure he'd support their position.

Of course, W, being a Compassionate Conservative, really has the best interests of working folks at heart when he opposes increasing the minimum wage. When he was asked if he supported an increase in the federal minimum wage, Bush said, "That's up to the Congress. I think it's important to do that in certain markets. What I worry about though is, is pricing people out of work."[5] What would folks do with all that extra money if we did raise the minimum wage? Probably just blow it on luxuries like baby food and diapers and rent. W's not like those old Cro-Magnon conservatives who were against the minimum wage because they hated the poor and wanted to keep them desperate so that businesses could exploit them. Bush is against the minimum wage because he loves the poor.

It's just that sometimes you have to hurt the ones you love.

Abraham Lincoln—a Republican who truly did care about the poor—once said, "The Good Lord must have loved common people; He made so many of them." And the Lord certainly placed a lot of hardworking minimum-wage-earning folks in Texas. It has the second highest number of workers—more than one million—who would benefit from an increase in the federal minimum wage. To be precise, Texas has 1,015,724 workers who could've used the raise, second only to California.[6] I don't know about you, but if Texas had more than a million billionaires who wanted to line their pockets with another outrageous Bush special-interest tax cut, I have a feeling I know where Bush would be.

He May Not Like Working People, But He Sure Likes Their Funds

In the 1999 legislative session, Bush called for legislation to take $400 million out of the Texas Workers Compensation Fund and place it in the state's general revenue fund, where it could be used for—you guessed it?—tax breaks for the more affluent. I gotta hand it to W, at least he's consistent.[7]

Back in 1994, when he was running for governor, W pledged to protect the state's teacher retirement fund from a similar raid. "I will oppose any effort to reduce contributions to the Teacher Retirement System or decrease the state's contribution rate," Bush's 1994 campaign literature said.

Oops.

In 1995, Bush cut $400 million in funding from the Teacher Retirement System, reducing the state contribution from 7.31 percent to 6 percent.[8]

Perhaps recalling the joy of those college panty raids, W went back for one more raid on the teachers' retirement system. In 1997 he tried to take $47 million from the teachers' pension fund and use it to pay for administrative costs that had heretofore been paid from general revenue.

The teachers, bless their little hearts, didn't like this. "We oppose the governor's raid of the $47 million in the teachers' retirement fund," said Texas State Teachers Association president Richard Kouri. "This is money that could be used to enhance the benefits of retirees or to enhance the benefits of active teachers."[9] Bush didn't care. If you could read his mind at the time (albeit a quick read), he was probably thinking: "So what if the teachers are mad? What do they know? They never ran a baseball team, they never worked in the oil bidness. If they're so dad-gum smart, they'd be governor, wouldn't they?"

Bush wanted to free up the $47 million in administrative costs for—if you're playing along at home you already know the answer—tax cuts for the more affluent. Gaaawd, I love this guy's consistency.

Look for the Anti-Union Label

Bush has been a strongly, stridently, anti-union governor. "I can't think of a single issue of substance on which he has been on our side," says AFL-CIO legal director Rick Levy. Not a single issue? Come on, Rick. Not all Republicans hate unions. I mean, Ronald Reagan was a union man—the president of a union, in fact. And Lech Walesa—the GOP loves Lech Walesa—used his Solidarity trade union to help tear down the Berlin Wall. Surely Bush must have found one instance, one issue, one teeny tiny matter on which he was willing to help working people.

So I went off in search of something, anything Bush has ever done to help the working people of his state protect themselves from corporate predators through their union.

Know what I found? Nada. Nuthin'. Zilch. Zip.

In 1999, when the police officers who work for Houston's Metropolitan Transit Authority wanted the right to form a union, the Texas Legislature (not exactly a hotbed of pro-union sentiment itself) passed a little ol' bill that would have allowed them to form a union, but not to strike, and not even to have full collective bargaining rights. Not exactly radical socialism.

Bush vetoed it.[10]

In 1997, the Legislature passed a bill to protect jobs by preventing employers from firing full-time workers and replacing them with temporary workers in taxpayer-subsidized welfare-to-work programs. The bill would also have applied federal worker protections such as the Fair Labor Standards Act and the minimum wage to Texans moving from welfare to work.

Bush vetoed it.[11]

Just as I was about to despair, I found out about a labor-oriented bill that Bush had signed. Apparently, back in 1995, as part of Texas' welfare reform, the state created the Texas Workforce Commission, to replace the Texas Employment Commission and coordinate job training and employment programs.

Then I learned why Bush signed it. "From its inception, the Texas Workforce Commission has focused solely on what is good for employers, not the work force," said Texas AFL-CIO president Joe Gunn. "In this agency, and in the Bush Administration, the boss always wins and the Number One workforce priority is cheap, compliant labor."[12]

And what, pray tell, could be wrong with that? Well, even if that were your priority, you'd be disappointed to learn Bush's buddies weren't handling the commission's funds very well. In 1999, the Texas state auditor released a report criticizing the commission for placing state and federal funds at risk because of inadequate oversight and poor monitoring of the way local workforce development boards award contracts related to the state's welfare reform initiatives. The state auditor's report concluded that up to $830 million in federal and state funds was being put at risk by the commission. The audit identified at least thirteen separate incidents in which the board mishandled the awarding of local service contracts. Remember, as one newspaper pointed out:

Bush "championed creation of the agency." He ought to be accountable for its alleged mismanagement.[13]

It's bad enough that Texas under George W. Bush treats working people like something a rancher scrapes off his boots. But it's another thing entirely to brag about it. Former President Bush was famous for reminding audiences of how his mother always told him not to be a "braggadocio." But W apparently doesn't have that same reticence—especially when it comes to bragging on how poorly his state treats its working people.

Bush's Texas Department of Economic Development brags about the state's anti-labor attitude. A TDED fact sheet described Texas' "Pro-Business Environment" (remember, that's pronounced "bid-ness"), saying "Texas is a right-to-work state, with low unionization of the manufacturing work force." The Web site also points out initiatives that have lowered employers' costs and the fact that working Texans make lower than average manufacturing wages.[14] What a great slogan: "Texas: We Treat Our Workers Like Dirt." (I cleaned up that last word a little in case any of you dear readers are young and impressionable.)

The Bottom Line

By now you're starting to get the notion that I don't like ol' W. Nothing could be further from the truth. I like the guy, but I can't stand what he's done. He opposes the minimum wage, stops efforts to protect full-time workers from being fired and replaced by subsidized welfare workers, messes with workers' compensation and pension funds, then brags about how crummy his state is to working people. What's compassionate about that?

I worked my way through college in part by holding down blue-collar jobs. I worked in a factory in Houston, heat-treating oilfield equipment in furnaces. I also worked in an oilfield warehouse in Channelview, Texas, for an offshore drilling outfit named Zapata. Turns out Zapata was started by W's Poppy. The factory workers and warehousemen I worked with were good people. They did hot, dangerous, boring work for faceless, nameless corporate big shots who didn't give a damn about them. The factory I worked in was closed down in the Reagan-Bush recession. There's a stereo superstore there now.

And now that the Clinton-Gore economy has working people finally making a decent living, I am not going to sit idly by and let Bush b.s. those folks into voting against their economic self-interest. I'll admit that most of the guys I worked with in the factory or the warehouse or at Court's Hardware in Stafford, Texas, would probably rather go to Al's Barbecue (with the sign over the door: "Tender as a Woman's Heart"), with W than the ever-serious Al Gore. But the presidency ain't about eatin' barbecue. It's about fighting entrenched power on behalf of the folks who have none. Bush thinks he's putting one over on you. That if he keeps up his line of jive you'll think he'll make a good president.

But you know better. You're reading this book. As we say in Texas, "Don't pee on my boots and tell me it's raining."

chapter 10

Is There an HMO Bureaucrat in the House?

"Well, there'll be a health care debate, and there'll be a health care issue that I'm going to, I mean, a health care speech and policy that I lay out. I talk about health care all the time at these one-on-ones when asked. It's on people's minds."

(CNN interview, 3/8/00)

"I'm sorry. I wish I could wave a wand."

(To the mother of a boy with a chronic, life-threatening illness whose medical insurance did not cover her child's needs, who had asked Bush what he was going to do about such cases, *New York Times*, 2/18/00)

Patients' Rights: Bush Is Wrong

Although he cynically brags on the campaign trail about Texas' patient protection law, Bush vigorously opposed that law. His Web site says, "Under Governor Bush, Texas enacted some of the most comprehensive patient protection laws in the nation." [1]

Bull.

In 1995, Bush vetoed the Patient Protection Act. The bill would have created rules punishing HMOs that: 1) fail to pay for emergency room visits or new treatments, 2) fire doctors without reason, or 3) encourage doctors to deny patients expensive treatment. The bill would also have given HMO customers the right to pay for coverage that allowed them to choose their own doctors. Bush said he vetoed the bill because it interfered with the market and increased costs. After the veto, Bush said, "It was the easy thing politically to sign the bill and the headline of your story ought to read, 'Governor shows political courage.' "[2]

The guy caves in to the HMO heavyweights and the insurance company lobbyists and he wants us to write a new chapter about him in *Profiles in Courage*. (It's a book, Governor. Karl Rove will explain it to you.)

In 1997, the Legislature took another run at patients' rights. And this bill was even stronger. The Managed Care Responsibility Act allowed Texans to sue their HMOs for medical malpractice. It passed the Legislature by a veto-proof margin. This put W in a pickle. He hated the bill. His rich backers in the HMO and insurance lobbies hated the bill. But he knew if he vetoed it, the Legislature would simply override him, and the already puny powers of the governor's office would be eroded.

Bush attacked the bill, saying, "I am concerned that this legislation has the potential to drive up health care costs and increase the number of lawsuits." But since a veto wasn't a viable option, he exercised a provision in the state constitution that allows bills to become law without the governor's signature.[3]

Now, what do you call it when a politician vetoes a bill, then attacks its successor legislation, then refuses to sign it—and then brags about it? In Texas we call that chutzpah. (It's Yiddish, Governor. Karl Rove will explain it to you.)

If he ever gets to Washington, you can bet Bush will continue to be a shameless suck-up to the big insurance companies and the HMOs. During the Senate debate on the Patients' Bill of Rights, Bush announced his support for the watered-down GOP version of health care "reform." The final GOP Senate bill would have applied to only 2 percent of employers—covering only 48 million Americans—as opposed to the Democratic plan, which would have protected 161 million Americans. The Republican bill Bush supported also prevented patients from being able to hold HMOs accountable for mistakes, allowed HMOs rather than doctors to determine what is medically necessary, prevented women from naming their OB-GYN as their primary physician, would only require emergency room care for federally regulated plans, and prevented most patients from being able to keep the same doctor for a few months if they have to switch health plans.[4]

Ending Medicare as We Know It

George W. Bush would end Medicare as we know it. He has not offered a plan of his own, but has said he wants to build on a controversial plan that would replace the Medicare system we now have with a voucher-based system through which seniors would purchase their own health care plans—without any firm guarantee that the current level of Medicare benefits would be maintained.[5] Medicare's chief actuary says the plan Bush supports could increase Medicare premiums by as much as 47 percent. Such an increase in premiums will pressure more and more seniors into joining HMOs.[6]

The plan Bush supports also raises the eligibility age for Medicare to sixty-seven, despite the fact that the most rapidly growing group of uninsured citizens are those ages fifty-five to sixty-five.[7]

So that's what Bush supports for Medicare. Now let's look at what he opposes: a guaranteed prescription drug benefit as part of the Medicare program. Instead, Bush supports a proposal to coerce seniors into HMOs in order to have access to prescription drug coverage.[8] Seniors with incomes of up to $22,500 per couple would get some subsidies under the Bush plan,[9] but nearly half the seniors who have no prescription drug coverage have incomes too high to get a meaningful subsidy from the skimpy, wimpy Bush plan.[10]

So, if you're a senior who needs prescription drug coverage, and you don't qualify for Bush's low-income subsidy, you're out of luck. Unless you "choose" to go into an HMO. Bush dresses this up by saying he wants to give seniors more options and choices. Some option. Some choice. Under the Bush plan, seniors would have the option of choosing a managed care plan that includes a prescription drug benefit, but that also has all the hassles and headaches that go with managed care.[11]

I think Bush is a big, fat phony on prescription drugs. I think he'd be happy to let half the seniors in America do without prescription drug coverage, even if it means forcing them to choose between paying the rent and paying for their medicine. But in his desire to buffalo seniors into thinking he's a "new kind of Republican" (kind of like a new kind of rattlesnake), he has embraced a plan that can't work in the real world, but that he's hoping will work in the campaign.

How do I know this? The numbers tell the story. Bush has not put his money where his plan is. That is, he has not committed to allocating the extra money needed to pay for a meaningful prescription drug plan. As the *Los Angeles Times* reported, "the absence of new money leads critics to suggest that the Bush plan could end up giving the elderly less than it appears to promise. . . . Even supporters of the Bush approach say that lack of additional funding is a serious omission. It's hard to imagine adding prescription drug coverage and covering the 78 million baby boomers who are retiring and not needing more money. . . . Anyone who says you don't is just not realistic," said Gail Wilensky, chairwoman of the Medicare Payment Advisory Commission and an administrator of the Health Care Financing Administration under former President Bush. "Maybe it will work in the short term, but not in the long term." [12]

But of course, it doesn't have to work in the long term. It just has to get him through the campaign. The Compassionate Conservative is really just a con artist.

Bush: People Choose to Be Uninsured

Texas leads the nation in the percentage of its residents who lack health insurance.[13] That's not necessarily George W. Bush's fault. Texas is a state with a long tradition of limited, inactive government, so I'm not willing to blame Bush for how Texas ranks on every sociopolitical problem. But it is fair to blame Bush for the specific things he has done as governor. Not what he's inherited, but what he has done—and what he has failed to do.

In a jaw-dropping statement that gives us a good sense of how his mind works (and I use that verb loosely), Bush said, "For those that are uninsured, many of the uninsured are able-bodied capable people capable of buying insurance but choose not to do so." [14]

Sure, W, just like the homeless choose to sleep on grates. People think through their options, and decide they want to be vulnerable, they want to rely on emergency care, they want to get sicker quicker, die younger, and see their kids suffer. Sure they do. And that's part of what's great about America: the freedom to endanger your children, suffer more, and die young. I just thank God we have a man like you who's willing to stand up and defend those precious rights.

If it's such a rational choice to choose to be uninsured, why doesn't Bush do it? Because he's got terrific government-supplied health care. He just doesn't want you to have what he's got. Must be nice to have a job in which the hired help have better benefits than the boss.

Perhaps because he thinks doing nothing is the best policy, Bush's sins on health coverage have been largely sins of omission. But in the area of health coverage, neglect can be deadly. According to the *New York Times:*

> Texas has had one of the nation's worst public health records for decades. More than a quarter of its residents have no health insurance. Its Mexican border is a hotbed of contagion. The state ranks near the top in the nation in rates of AIDS, diabetes, tuberculosis and teenage pregnancy, and near the bottom in immunizations, mammograms and access to physicians. But since George W. Bush became governor in 1995, he has not made health a priority, his aides acknowledge. He has never made a speech on the subject, his press office says. His administration opposed a patient's bill of rights in 1995 before grudgingly accepting one in 1997, and fought unsuccessfully to limit access to the new federal Children's Health Insurance Program in 1999.[15]

The *Times* has it right. We can't blame Bush for Texas' decades-old problems. But we have a right to hold him accountable for his shocking indifference to one of the most important problems his state faces. His inattention to the problem displays a callousness at odds with the wise-cracking, smiling (okay, smirking) persona we see on the campaign trail. You'd think someone who'd led such a charmed life would be especially attuned to the suffering of others. That's the way FDR and JFK were. And that's the way Al Gore is.

But not our George. When a woman approached him in Florence, South Carolina, and told him the heartbreaking story of her son's life-threatening disease, and how her medical insurance didn't cover what he needed, Bush blathered on about medical savings accounts—basically health insurance policies with a $3,000 to $4,000 deductible. Then, realizing it was a little late for this woman with a critically ill child to open a medical savings account, he dismissed her. "I'm sorry," he said. "I wish I could wave a wand." [16]

I'll bet if a rich woman had come up to Bush, complaining that her biggest worry was how she could leave more of her money to her lazy, shiftless son, Bush would wave a magic wand. He'd tell her he supports complete repeal of the millionaire's inheritance tax. Too bad for this woman that she wanted something frivolous—like lifesaving medical care—for her son.

It's all about priorities, and W seems to have figured that out. If you whip out your checkbook to write a trillion-dollar tax break for the rich, you don't have the "magic wand" to create universal health care.

What sense of entitlement makes someone so callous and cold-hearted? Even if he hadn't had the policy solution at his fingertips, you can imagine Ronald Reagan taking her in his arms and comforting her, or Bill Clinton famously feeling her pain. Each from their own side of the ideological spectrum, Reagan and Clinton gave a damn about real people. Bush seems to have developed the cynical and savage motto of his mentor, the late Lee Atwater, "It's all b.s."

But it's not all b.s., Governor. It's life and death for some people. Especially children.

Bush Fought Against Expanding Children's Health Insurance

Texas has 1.4 million children with no health insurance. So you would think that when President Clinton created the Children's Health Insurance Program (CHIP)—which provides health insurance for children in families that don't qualify for Medicaid and can't afford private insurance—and got the Republican Congress to pass it into law, Bush would treat it as a godsend. Instead, he saw it as a pain in the ass. Even though one out of four children in his state have no health insurance, Bush fought efforts to expand CHIP.[17]

Bush's initial 1999 budget proposal funded CHIP at such a low level that 220,000 poor children would have been left out of the plan.[18] But under pressure from Democrats—and clearly with an eye toward the 2000 presidential election—Bush finally agreed to a Democratic proposal to cover more children. At the signing ceremony Bush privately told one of the bill's supporters, the lionhearted Austin Democratic state representative Glen Maxey, "You crammed it down our throats."[19]

What kind of a man could be so bitter about helping poor children get medical care? The kind of man who's never had to worry about paying for health care for his own children.

Now that you know how Bush opposed that CHIP program, which aids families slightly above the poverty line, you can imagine how hostile he is to the Medicaid program that cares for the really poor. Federal officials are investigating why nearly 600,000 children in Texas who are eligible for Medicaid are not enrolled. Experts say Texas puts up roadblocks, and parents don't realize their children are still eligible for Medicaid after the family leaves welfare. "Texas' public policy is at times notably unfavorable to improving access to Medicaid for children in families at or below poverty," said Anne Dunkelberg, a senior policy analyst at the nonprofit Center for Public Policy Priorities in Austin. "In most cases, this has occurred because families leaving [welfare] have no idea that their children can continue on Medicaid at much higher incomes than those allowed for [welfare]."[20]

Medicaid experts said Texas could enroll more poor children in the health care program if the process were less cumbersome. Texas is one of only eleven states that require applicants to pass an assets test, where they must bring written proof of bank accounts, savings, and the value of their cars, rather than just income. Experts also say the six-month eligibility review, which requires a two-hour visit during business hours, could be done by mail or phone to help recipients.[21]

What a Surprise! Bush's Health Care Plan Good for the Rich, Terrible for the Rest

Pop quiz: What's the single biggest reason people don't have health insurance? They can't afford it, of course. Bush's solution is—you're going to love this—cut taxes. You get the sense that if someone broke their leg, Bush would advise them to take two tax cuts and call him in the morning. As the health care advocates at Families USA point out, Bush has proposed a tax credit of $2,000 per family to help people pay for health insurance. Trouble is, it's a shell game. A typical family health insurance plan runs $5,000 to $6,000 a year, which means a family that can't afford health care still has to come up with $3,000 or $4,000 (10 percent of their income if they're around the national median income). No wonder Families USA calls Bush's proposal "a trivial response to a serious problem."[22]

Bush's call for medical savings accounts (MSAs) is another example of Bush prescribing tax cuts for every ailment. MSAs are great—if you're healthy and wealthy (like Bush). But if you're not, they're of no help. They are basically a tax shelter for rich people, allowing them to save money, tax-free, for medical expenses. Most proposals allow you to set aside $5,000 in such shelters. If you don't spend it on medical care, you can keep it. Now, if you have an extra five grand lying around, these are for you. But if you don't, MSAs wind up being an insurance policy with a deductible of $3,000 to $4,000. Some deal.

But if you are healthy and wealthy they are a good deal. Experts say MSAs would only help about 10,000 people out of the 44.3 million who lack health insurance. But for those 10,000 they're great. They allow you to shelter more income from taxes, and still protect you against catastrophic risk. So what's the harm? If you cherry-pick the healthy and wealthy out of the health insurance pool, you wind up raising premiums for the rest of us[23]—and cost the government about $4 billion in tax subsidies.[24]

So once again Bush has a proposal that would hurt the middle class and the poor, while helping the rich. How can you not admire this man's genius?

Bottom Line

Bush's real plan for health care is this: Plan not to get sick. His plan for Medicare? Plan not to grow old. His plan for you if you're in a bureaucratic, unresponsive HMO? Plan to wait a long time—just to be told no.

chapter 11

The Grim Reaper Wore a Smirk:
Bush and the Death Penalty

"This case has had full analyzation and has been looked at a lot. I understand the emotionality of death penalty cases."

(Seattle Post-Intelligencer, 6/23/00)

"The only things that I can tell you is that every case I have reviewed I have been comfortable with the innocence or guilt of the person that I've looked at. I do not believe we've put a guilty . . . I mean innocent person to death in the state of Texas."

(National Public Radio, 6/22/00)

"Please don't kill me!"

(Mocking the voice of Karla Faye Tucker; Bush in fact allowed her execution to go forward, despite pleas from Christian leaders, *Boston Herald,* 11/18/99)

On February 3, 1998, the state of Texas executed Karla Faye Tucker. Tucker was a pickax murderer. There was no doubt about her guilt. But Bush was besieged by politically influential Christian conservatives, including the Reverend Pat Robertson, to spare her life because she had undergone a religious transformation.

Tucker's gender made the case unusual, but it was Bush's mocking of her last, desperate plea for life that made the case infamous. In an interview with conservative journalist Tucker Carlson, Bush was asked if he'd ever spoken with Karla Faye. He said he had not, that he'd seen no point in talking to her. Then, imagining what she might have said, Bush twisted his face into a sneer and mimicked Karla Faye's voice, saying, "Please don't kill me!"[1]

A firestorm ensued, and rather than simply apologizing for such a callous, cavalier, cynical, heartless attitude about the taking of a human life, Bush did what a lifetime of frat-boy pranks had taught him to do: he denied it. In fact, he hit the home run of chickenhearted Bush excuses:

First Base: You're Taking It Out of Context. Bush spokesperson Karen Hughes said Carlson had "misread the governor" during some of his conversations.[2]

Second Base: We Were Off the Record. According to the *Washington Post*, "The Bush campaign has said that his conversations with author Tucker Carlson were either off the record or taken out of context."[3]

Third Base: I Don't Remember Saying That. Regarding Bush's generous use of the f-word in that same interview, Hughes said neither Bush nor any staff members recalled Bush using foul language, but said it was inappropriate if he did.[4]

Home Plate: It Depends on What the Meaning of "Interview" Is. The candidate himself came down with a frightening case of amnesia regarding the Carlson interview. "I didn't do the interview for *Talk,*" Bush said. "It wasn't an interview." In Bush's view, the conversation with Carlson was "Somebody coming to get a flavor of the campaign. It wasn't a sit-down interview." Asked to describe the difference, Bush paused until his spokesperson rescued him by calling out in a loud voice, "Governor, you need to get back to your guests."[5]

Even if you support the death penalty, this behavior raises questions about character. But lest you think this is an isolated instance, let me give you another example of Bush's appalling lack of respect for human life.

What Are You Laughing at, George?

On March 2, in a GOP debate in Los Angeles, CNN's Jeff Greenfield asked Bush a question about the rash of "sleeping lawyer" cases—

cases in which defendants in Texas have been sentenced to death despite the fact that their lawyer had slept through the trial. As Greenfield was asking the question, Bush chuckled noticeably. (Here is where print is limited. I have seen the videotape of that debate a number of times, and I've replayed it on *Equal Time*. There is no doubt that Bush is laughing.)[6]

What's so funny about lawyers sleeping while their clients are on trial for their lives? You'll have to ask W. To me, that's not funny; that's sick.

Bush and Sleeping Lawyer Syndrome

In 1997, *The Nation* called sleeping lawyer capital cases a "bona fide trend." The Texas Court of Appeals regularly turns down petitions from death row inmates whose lawyers slept through significant portions of their trials or provided ineffective or incompetent counsel. A few examples include:

- In 1996, Texas executed Carl Johnson. According to Johnson's appeals lawyer, the original trial lawyer had slept "during jury selection and portions of the testimony itself," and was later disciplined for incompetence in another death penalty case.[7]

- In 1996, the Texas Court of Criminal Appeals, by a 7 to 2 decision, agreed that the lead lawyer's sleeping and loud snoring did not violate defendant George McFarland's Sixth Amendment right to effective, competent counsel and there was therefore no reason to reopen the case. The decision stated that assistant counsel's decision to allow the lead attorney to sleep could be viewed—get this—"as a strategic move on his part." Now there's a helluva strategy: sleep through the trial.[8]

- In 1983, Calvin Burdine was sentenced to death in Texas after his court-appointed attorney slept through much of the trial. Three jurors and the former court clerk testified they saw Burdine's lawyer sleeping. One observer said that during testimony the lawyer "became bored or sleepy and fell asleep, or raised no objections to any of the questions that were being asked the witnesses by the district attorney." The Texas Court of Criminal Appeals denied Burdine's appeal for a new trial on the grounds that the lawyer's sleeping did not affect the jury's verdict. On April 11, just hours before he was scheduled to be executed, U.S. District Judge David Hittner overruled the Texas court's decision and stayed the execution.[9] (This, by the way, was the specific case that Greenfield was asking Bush about. Why it prompted smirks and guffaws is beyond me.)

Under Bush's leadership, the Texas courts have barely batted an eye at these sleeping lawyer cases. In fact, one judge said, "The Constitution doesn't say the lawyer has to be awake."[10] But wouldn't it help? Maybe Bush doesn't care about this because he slept through so many classes in school, and still went on to become rich and powerful.

Bush Vetoed a Bill to Improve Lawyers for Impoverished Defendants

In 1999 Bush vetoed a perfectly useful little bill that would have taken a few small steps toward ensuring that poor people aren't sent to prison—or the death chamber—because of poor lawyers. The bill, which passed the notoriously tough-on-crime Texas Legislature unanimously, would have set a twenty-day deadline for appointing a public defender, so court-appointed lawyers would have time to prepare a defense, and defendants would have legal counsel sooner. (Most states require that a lawyer be appointed within seventy-two hours.)[11] The bill also would have instituted various other improvements on how lawyers are assigned to poor defendants.[12]

It was hardly a radical proposal. And when Bush was first asked about it, he didn't know a thing in the world about it. "Before I stake my claim I want to make sure I understand what it says. But could you explain the bill?" The bill's sponsor broke in and said that he and Bush would have to sit down and go over the details. Another reporter reminded Bush that he had said he was going to put his presidential campaign on hold to focus on the Legislature, but that perhaps his ignorance of this bill suggested he wasn't doing so. Bush replied, "I was focused, but I don't know this particular bill. . . . This is the first I have heard of the bill."[13]

But it wasn't the last. Judges are elected in Texas, and are a potent political force. They made sure Bush knew they didn't like this little ol' bill one bit. Linda Edwards, a Bush spokesperson, said their office had "received more than 100 phone calls and faxes from judges and others expressing their concerns about the legislation." [14]

So here is another potentially life-or-death issue on which Bush has to make a decision. The kind of decision a president makes every day. Do I protect potentially innocent lives, and risk annoying a powerful political constituency? Or do I suck up to power?

Anybody want to guess what Bush did? You got it. He vetoed that sucker.

In his veto message, the Compassionate One said, "While well-intentioned, the effect of the bill is likely to be neither better representation for indigents nor a more efficient administration of justice." [15] You see: he killed the bill for the good of the poor. That's real compassion.

Oh, sure, the whiny babies started bitching about it. Joe Sanchez of the Mexican-American Legal Defense and Education Fund contrasted the veto with Bush's signing of emergency legislation to help the oil industry, saying, "He is showing his conservatism to the poor and his compassion to the rich." And Stephen B. Bright, director of the Southern Center for Human Rights in Atlanta, said, "Governor Bush's action on the bill is an important indicator of how much confidence we can have in his commitment to equal justice for the poor, racial minorities and other disadvantaged persons." [16]

Oh, dry up. It took courage for Bush to stand up to some of the poorest people in our society. Anybody can take the easy way out, and suck up to the powerful poor people's lobby. It takes a real he-man to railroad the poor into prison and the death chamber. Come to think of it, the same kind of he-man it takes to execute a woman and then laugh about it.

At Least He's Consistent: Kill 'Em All, Let God Sort 'Em Out!

According to Amnesty International USA, the state of Texas executes almost as many people per month as such bastions of enlightenment as Iran, Iraq, and Saudi Arabia. Bush has presided over 135 executions as of this writing, and he's scheduled to average about a killing a week between now and the election.[17]

And there's no age discrimination when Texas kills. In the entire nation there have been sixteen people executed for crimes they committed as juveniles. Texas alone has executed eight of them. Dozens of other men are on death row for crimes they committed while they were still juveniles.[18]

And now that Bush has signed the "Speed Up the Juice Law," maybe he'll even be able to execute someone while he's still a juvenile. In 1995 Bush signed the aptly named law, which limits the appeals process for death row inmates. The bill required habeas corpus appeals (which address constitutional questions) and direct appeals (which challenge trial procedures) to be filed at the same time. In the past, such appeals were separated, with most lawyers giving priority to direct appeals, since they are more likely to involve issues of guilt or innocence.

Opponents of the bill said shortening appeals increased the likelihood of executing an innocent person. Since the law was passed, the average length of time a Texas inmate spends on death row has gone from nine years to four and a half years. "[We're] confident that in the long run the death row appeals process will be streamlined and that the time between conviction and execution will be significantly shortened," said a Bush spokesman when asked about the law.[19] So will the time needed to discover a mistake, W. But maybe that's the point. In the Texas death machine, we bury our mistakes.

Bush Opposed Bill Banning Execution of the Mentally Retarded

You'd think W would have a soft spot for the mentally challenged. But just last year, Bush said he opposed a bill that would prohibit the execution of the mentally retarded, and said, "That's up to juries to decide. I like the law the way it is now."[20]

Ronald Reagan didn't believe in executing the mentally retarded. He signed a law barring the federal government from executing the mentally retarded. And W's brother, Florida Governor Jeb Bush says, "People with clear mental retardation should not be executed."[21] I guess Reagan and Jeb are more . . . well . . . compassionate conservatives.

Viva Las Vegas! Too Busy Raising Money to Make a Phone Call to Save a Life

Even the one case in which Bush did ask for a reprieve is illustrative of his callous and hard-hearted approach to his role in the Texas death machine. On May 18, 2000, Bush signed a death warrant for Ricky McGinn. Two weeks later, on May 31, 2000, he called for a reprieve.[22] No facts had changed, no new evidence had come to light, no new arguments had been made. The only difference was the Ricky McGinn case was making headlines.

Why do you suppose Bush changed his position? A Bush defender would say that perhaps he'd reexamined the record. Maybe a pang of conscience. Nope. In fact, Bush that day attended a fund-raiser in Las Vegas[23] and campaigned in California. Bush didn't even officially grant the reprieve, a task which fell to State Senator Rodney Ellis, who was acting governor in the absence of both Bush and Lieutenant Governor Rick Perry.[24]

If someone's life were in your hands, and you thought he should get a reprieve, wouldn't you take a minute from your swinging Las Vegas shindig to make a phone call to ensure that the execution didn't go through? Ahh, but you are not George W. Bush, graduate of the Harvard Business School, where they teach that delegating is the essence of good management. Even delegating death.

The Bottom Line

Bush's chief of staff told the *Los Angeles Times* that, four months into his term, Bush shortened the amount of time he reviews each death penalty case from thirty minutes to just fifteen.[25]

Fifteen minutes to make a life or death decision. Fifteen minutes. He spent weeks polishing his convention speech. He spends three and a half hours *a day* working out, playing video games, and napping. But he can't spare more than fifteen minutes—half the time it takes to watch *The Dukes of Hazzard*—to decide whether a fellow human being lives or dies.

Bush was asked during a news conference whether it was acceptable that innocent people be put to death. "No, it's not acceptable, and under my watch, I'm telling you that I've analyzed every case, and I don't believe that's the case. I'm confident that it's not the case—that the people who have been put to death have been guilty of the crime charged, and have had full access to the courts."[26]

Curious. As an anti-big-government conservative, W is deeply, reflexively skeptical of government. He does not trust the government to write a national health plan, for example. Or to extend Medicare to cover prescription drugs. Or even to fully run Social Security—hence his plan to partially privatize it.

But when the issue is the life or death of a human being, Bush suddenly exhibits a faith in government that is truly inspiring. He believes that even sleeping, court-appointed lawyers are competent, that juries never err (unless they're slapping punitive damages on a big corporation), and that the bureaucracy of death is more reliable than the bureaucracy of public education. So reliable, in fact, that it is perfect.

And he's willing to bet your life on it.

chapter 12

Bush and Race: "Porch Monkeys," Bob Jones, and the Confederate Flag

"What I am against is quotas. I am against hard quotas. Quotas they basically delineate based upon whatever. However they delineate, quotas, I think vulcanize society. So I don't know how that fits into what everybody else is saying, their relative positions, but that's my position."

(*San Francisco Chronicle*, 1/21/00)

"That school was based upon the Bible."

(Describing Bob Jones University, *Palm Beach Post*, 2/4/00)

"I do not agree with this notion that somehow if I go to try to attract votes and to lead people toward a better tomorrow somehow I get subscribed to some—some doctrine gets subscribed to me."

(Trying again to defend his appearance at Bob Jones University, *Meet the Press*, 2/13/00)

"I don't have to accept their tenets. I was trying to convince those college students to accept my tenets. And I reject any labeling me because I happened to go to the university."

(Trying once more to defend his appearance at Bob Jones University, *Today*, 2/23/00)

When Hate Came to Texas, Where Was George?

When James Byrd, Jr., was brutally murdered—lynched by being dragged from the back of a pickup truck until his body literally came apart—just for being black, it was one of the most shocking crimes in Texas history. The small town of Jasper, Texas, was stunned. Civil rights leaders like the Reverend Jesse Jackson and political leaders like Texas Republican Senator Kay Bailey Hutchison rushed to Jasper to calm the community and comfort the family.

But where was George?

The man who has held so many photo ops with African-American children abandoned his fellow Texans when they needed him most. Bush's absence from Jasper stands in stark contrast to his reaction when seven white Christians were gunned down in a church in Fort Worth. He was campaigning in Minnesota at the time, but Bush flew home to be there.

Why would the governor of Texas fly across the country to comfort white families when he wouldn't drive halfway across the state to comfort black families?

Bush abandoned the African-American community again when the James Byrd, Jr., Hate Crimes Act was before the Texas Legislature. Daryl Verrett, the nephew of James Byrd, Jr., asked Bush to support the legislation. "I asked him personally if he would use his influence to help pass the bill. . . . He told me, 'No.' "[1]

Bush's excuse for opposing the hate crimes legislation is lame. "I've always said every crime is a hate crime. People, when they commit a crime, have hate in their heart. It's hard to distinguish between one degree of hate and another."[2]

Nonsense.

Bush's line of argument shows his facility for the sound bite ("every crime is a hate crime") and the vapidity of his brain. Of course every crime is not a hate crime. To say so is facile and stupid. Swiping a Christmas wreath from the door of a store as part of a college fraternity escapade, as he did thirty-four years ago,[3] is not a hate crime. It's just a childish prank, easily forgiven. Insider trading (which Bush came perilously close to committing) is not a crime of hate, it's a crime of greed. Killing a man in a barroom brawl is not the same as grabbing an innocent man walking down the street, chaining him to the back of a pickup truck, and dragging him to death. Targeting someone for violence because of their race, religion, gender, disability, or sexual orientation— that's a hate crime.

Bush says, "It's hard to distinguish between one degree of hate and another."

Garbage.

It's called motive, and it is determinative in many other areas of law. If I shoot and kill another man, is it murder? That depends on motive. If my motive in killing an enemy in combat is to do my duty as part of the armed forces, we rightly call that killing a patriotic act. If my motive is self-defense, we rightly call that killing justified. If my motive is to shoot a deer, and I accidentally shoot a man, it may simply be a tragic accident. But if my motive in pulling the trigger is to murder, then it's a crime. And in many states, if my motive for the murder itself is money, or to further some other felony, I can get the death penalty.

The same act, A shooting B, can have five different consequences—all based on motive. Whether I get a medal or the electric chair depends on motive.

We all know in our bones that the punishment for spray-painting "Go Longhorns" on a wall should be less than the punishment for spray-painting "Kill Jews." Both are wrongful acts, but only one is hateful. The motive matters.

When racists in the earlier part of this century lynched black men they were not only murdering, they were also attacking an entire community. And so we all recoil at the suffering of James Byrd, Jr. There were hundreds of murders in Texas in 1998, but that one stands out. Why? Because the racists who did it were trying to send a message of hate to the entire community.

And thus the community of civilized people has a responsibility to send a message as well: if your motive for killing, beating, lynching, or attacking is hatred directed at an entire community, we are going to ensure your swift and certain punishment.

It's a shame that Governor Bush refused to go to Jasper to comfort the Byrd family and heal the community. When character and courage called him to stand against hate—Bush hid.

The conservative philosopher Edmund Burke said, "All that is necessary for evil to triumph is for good men to do nothing." Bush is a good man. He has a good heart—especially on issues of race. And yet when political calculus—and political cowardice—dictated that he do nothing when he was naked to stand against evil, he did nothing.

Shame on him.

Bob Jones University

On February 2, 2000, Bush made his first campaign stop in South Carolina at Bob Jones University, a school known for its policy banning interracial dating. Bush defended his decision to speak at Bob Jones University two days after speaking there by saying "that school [Bob Jones] was based upon the Bible."[4] Bush wouldn't go to Jasper but he was happy to go to Bob Jones University.

At least W's South Carolina campaign manager was honest enough to admit why. He told *Newsweek* that Bush did not go there to persuade folks to turn away from racial and religious divisions. He went there "to build a wall between McCain and the social conservatives." In other words, to suck up to folks who believe interracial dating should be banned and the pope is an antichrist.[5]

They got the message. And so did we. The message we got was that, while far from prejudiced himself, Bush is shockingly comfortable in the presence of prejudice. As you may know, Bob Jones University has, shall we say, a colorful history:

According to a former student of Bob Jones University, the school president refused to fly the campus flag at half-mast after the Reverend Martin Luther King, Jr., was assassinated, and the president referred to King as an "apostate," one who had abandoned the Christian faith.[6]

The school lost its tax-exempt status in 1970 for refusing to admit African-Americans. The school then changed its policy but still prohibited any interracial dating or marriage.

During a 1982 address in Iowa, then chancellor Bob Jones, Jr., defended Bob Jones University's rule barring interracial dating. Although the school was integrated in the 1970s, in 1982 it had only about a dozen African-Americans. According to Jones, Jr., "blacks aren't attracted to fundamentalism, and they don't like discipline."[7]

In 1983, the U.S. Supreme Court again supported an IRS decision to remove tax-exempt status from the school for its dating policy, which included rules such as "students who date outside their own race will be expelled."[8]

In March 2000, university president Bob Jones III announced that the school had abandoned its interracial dating policy, partially due to the attention the school had received since Bush's visit there.[9] I salute Bob Jones for abandoning—albeit belatedly—its racially discriminatory policy. But the school defiantly continues to preach a rather nasty brand of anti-Catholic bigotry.

The Reverend Bob Jones has called the pope "an antichrist" who "brings a curse wherever he goes."[10] The university's Web site includes a "Message from the President," Bob Jones himself, which describes both the Catholic and Mormon faiths as cults.[11] Bob Jones University Press published a fifth-grade social studies textbook entitled *Heritage Studies for Christian Schools* used by fundamentalist schools around the country. The book describes Catholicism as a "false religion."[12]

All of this was well documented before Bush went there. He knew or should have known about the school. Bush claims he went to Bob Jones not to endorse its message of exclusion, but to tout his message of inclusion. No, W, that's what Alan Keyes did. Keyes went to Bob Jones and spoke as an African-American married to an Indian-American. He spoke as a Catholic. He spoke the truth to power. W, you just kissed butt.

Saluting the Confederate Flag

We Texans are not especially hung up on the Civil War. My friends from the Deep South call it "the War of Northern Aggression" and see much of their history and heritage through the distorted prism of that tragic experience.

Texans don't identify with losers. The Confederacy lost, and while Texas was a part of it, we did not have any of the crucial battles, nor did we produce any of the Confederacy's key leaders. We went along for the ride, largely, I suspect, because like our Southern neighbors Texas prospered from the sin of slavery. But we Texans haven't spent the last 135 years getting our panties in a wad over honoring the Lost Cause. As I said, we ain't much for honoring losers.

The Texas revolution looms large, and the mythic heroes of the Alamo are still our role models today. (Heck, one of my boys is named after the commander of the Alamo, William Travis, and I have nephews named after Stephen F. Austin and Sam Houston.) We have no need to venerate the racism of the Confederacy; we honor the heroism of the Republic of Texas.

Which is why I was so puzzled and angry over W's gutless performance on the issue of the Confederate flag flying over the state capitol in Columbia, South Carolina. Bush should have called a racist symbol by its name. But he didn't. He dodged and bobbed and weaved. He claimed states' rights. And even when an incredulous MSNBC's Brian Williams put him on the spot by asking him, "So, you have no reaction to the sight, as an American citizen, of that flag?" Bush replied, "No. Not in South Carolina, I do not."[13]

No. Not in South Carolina he doesn't. Bush knew he needed the votes of racists and bigots to stop the reform movement of John McCain. So he hid behind the state's right to offend and insult.

Of course, Bush doesn't believe the state of Oregon has the right to decide whether it can legalize physician-assisted suicide. He doesn't believe any state should have the right to allow legal abortions. So forgive me if I don't buy W's principled support for states' rights on the Confederate flag. Besides, to hear anyone using the states' rights argument to support racism sounds more like George Wallace than George W. Bush.

A Few (Not So) Good Men

In a candid admission of his own lack of ability and experience, W is forever assuring us that he'll have good people around him. (As if a competent, intelligent, experienced leader would not?) So it's fair to

look at what some of Bush's "good people" have had to say on the topic
of race and equality in America:

"Porch Monkeys," "Black Bastards," and "N***** Charlie"

One of the few powers the governor of Texas has is the power to nomi-
nate people to high-level state jobs. So when it came time to appoint
someone to take charge of all of the training for the state's law enforcement personnel, the mighty Bush brain swung into action. Of all the
people he could have chosen, Bush decided the best man for the job
was the police chief of Marshall, Texas, Charles W. Williams. So in November 1999, W elevated Chief Williams to chairman of the Texas
Commission on Law Enforcement Standards and Education. A year before W made him chairman, Chief Williams had testified in a discrimination lawsuit that the terms "porch monkeys" and "black bastard"
were not racial slurs. "If it's a general statement, no, I don't consider it
a racial slur," Williams said.[14]

As recently as April 6 of this year, Williams continued to defend
his remarks. When asked by the Associated Press about his comments,
Williams said, "You just have to show me where it's a racial slur. It just
depends on how it's used and who it's used toward."[15]

And it gets worse. According to the Associated Press, Williams was
asked in the same deposition about the "n-word." He stressed that he
only used that word in advising others never to use it. But he also said
that as a child fifty years ago in Oklahoma that word was used often, and
that black people then didn't mind. "I was born and raised with blacks,
and back then we had N***** Charlie and N***** Sam, N***** Joe,
and we regarded those people with all the respect in the world. That was
their name," said Williams. "They didn't mind. It wasn't any big deal
then," he added. "It graduated from that to Negro, then it graduated to
black, and now it's African-American. So to me that was not any different than me calling him an African-American today."[16]

Now, I don't know Chief Williams, and I have no interest in judging
him. I, too, can remember the n-word being used when I was a kid (and
I'm about twenty years younger than the chief). It was never used as a

term of respect. It was always used to demean, to denigrate, to dehumanize. I can also remember the side entrance to the Palms Theatre in Sugar Land, Texas. Folks who went through it went straight up to the balcony, while folks who used the front door went through the lobby. I remember asking why. Then someone told me that just above that side door they'd painted over the sign that used to say "Colored Entrance." Those words, those symbols, those insults, were all designed for a purpose. For someone to pretend otherwise is a sin against history.

Kinda makes you nervous about Bush making lifetime appointments, doesn't it?

Hispanics Don't Care About Unwed Pregnancies?

If Chief Williams was the only controversial appointee Bush had made, you might think I was making too much of it. But then again you probably don't know about Reyn Archer. Dr. William "Reyn" Archer is Bush's appointed health commissioner. He is also the son of Representative Bill Archer, the chairman of the powerful House Ways and Means Committee and the man who succeeded George Herbert Walker Bush in the House of Representatives. (I guess W has a soft spot for the moronic children of powerful politicians.) Dr. Archer is an MD, but he talks like a nutty professor. He once said that one cause of high teenage pregnancy rates in Texas is Hispanics' resistance to the notion that "getting pregnant is a bad thing."[17] Sure, Reyn.

As Ricky Ricardo used to say, you got a lot of 'splainin' to do, Reyn. Here's how he tries to explain it: "Society values pregnancies in teenagers as bad, but certain communities within society may feel differently. I think the Hispanic community generally thinks that pregnancy is a positive thing. They tend to be less judgmental toward a teenager who's pregnant than the Anglo or African-American communities."[18]

Dr. Doofus is also an equal opportunity offender. The *Houston Chronicle* reported that he had also made derogatory comments about African-Americans in a 1998 speech. Archer added that African-Americans were more loyal to each other, that he had seen cultures where loyalty is more important than honesty, and that blacks "don't buy" such cultural and legal institutions as marriage.[19]

Anything else, Doc? Well, yes, frankly, the *Chronicle* also reported that Archer said that loyalty could explain why a black jury thought O.J. Simpson was innocent when most white people do not, or why blacks are loyal to Jesse Jackson when they don't agree with him, and that "Anglos" were uninvited guests, perhaps, in their attempts to help the black community.[20]

The Bottom Line

I don't believe for one minute that George W. Bush is a racist. My sense of him is that he doesn't have a prejudiced bone in his body. But he sure seems mighty comfortable in the presence of prejudice. Just like his Poppy was willing to let an independent group exploit the racial angle of the Willie Horton case, Bush is happy to get the support of people who think the pope is an antichrist, or who call black people "porch monkeys," or think Hispanics don't care about teen pregnancy.

Jefferson said slavery in America was like a fire bell in the night. While Bush's heart is in the right place, his sense of political expediency has led him to cover his ears so he can't hear the fire bell.

chapter 13

Dan Quayle Without the Experience: Bush and Foreign Policy

"When I was coming up, it was a dangerous world, and you knew exactly who they were. It was us versus them, and it was clear who them was. Today, we are not so sure who the they are, but we know they're there."

(Iowa Western Community College, 1/21/00)

"This is still a dangerous world. It's a world of madmen and uncertainty and potential mental losses."

(South Carolina oyster roast, *Boston Globe,* 1/23/00)

"The only thing I know about Slovakia is what I learned first-hand from your foreign minister, who came to Texas."

(To a Slovak journalist; Bush had in fact met with the prime minister of Slovenia, not the foreign minister of Slovakia, Knight-Ridder News Service, 6/22/99)

"Keep good relations with the Grecians."

(*The Economist,* 6/12/99)

"If the East Timorians decide to revolt, I'm sure I'll have a statement."

(To Maureen Dowd, *New York Times,* 6/16/99)

"The fundamental question is, 'Will I be a successful President when it comes to foreign policy?' I will be, but until I'm the President it's going to be hard for me to verify that I think I'll be more effective."

(*New York Times,* 6/28/00)

"Bush said 'a key to foreign policy is to rely on reliance.' "

(Boston Globe, 1/23/00)

"There is madmen in the world, and there are terror."

(Associated Press, 2/16/00)

Why is it that Jacob Weisberg's wonderful list of Bushisms, which is updated weekly in the online magazine Slate.com, has so many examples of W tripping over himself when the topic turns to foreign policy?

Could it be because W doesn't know a dadgum thing about it? Didn't he even play a couple of games of Risk in college?

The Bushisms are hilarious. The idea of Bush being president is not so funny. Especially when you examine the things he's said about foreign and defense policy when his foot was not in his mouth. The post–Cold War world is certainly safer for America, thanks in large measure to the resolve of our military and the leadership of our president. But this is still a dangerous world. Twelve nations either have or are thought to be developing nuclear capability.[1] As many as twenty wars have raged recently in different trouble spots around the globe.[2] From the Middle East to Northern Ireland to the Balkans, America has made the difference between peace and war.

And into this complex cauldron stumbles George Walker Bush. Even one of his father's top foreign policy advisers, General Brent Scowcroft, confessed Bush wasn't comfortable with foreign affairs, claiming W's chief experience "was being around when his father was in his many different jobs. . . . Is he comfortable with foreign policy? I would say not."[3]

Perhaps the better question, General Scowcroft, is: Are we comfortable with W running the foreign policy of the only superpower on God's earth? I would say not.

And apparently, even W's chief foreign policy adviser is with me on this. Condoleezza Rice, the Stanford dean who is tutoring W, has this to say about her student: "He certainly doesn't have a great deal of foreign affairs experience." Poor Dr. Rice. I can imagine that, after teaching the brightest students in the country at Stanford, trying to teach this lunkhead, you feel like NASCAR star Bobby Labonte driving a go-cart. Preparation for the presidency should not be like remedial gym class, where you get credit for flopping on the mat. Mess up on the parallel bars and you get embarrassed. If W confuses the nuclear button with the TV remote, we lose the whole Eastern Seaboard.

And don't think he isn't capable of a monumental screwup. Although he lives closer to Mexico City than Washington, D.C., he didn't know what continent Mexico is part of.[4] He thought a plate of cheese fries was the prime minister of Canada. I'm not making this up. When a Canadian radio prankster congratulated him on being endorsed by "Prime Minister Poutin" of Canada, Bush thought it was on the level.[5] "Poutin" is basically a greasy plate of cheese fries. (Canada, Governor, is a large country just to the north of us. No, not Oklahoma, sir. Even farther north. Its prime minister is Jean Chretien, who bears no resemblance to a plate of cheese fries. And foreign leaders don't generally endorse in American elections.)

Even after his disastrous pop quiz on foreign leaders, he hadn't learned his lesson. He jokingly dared the moderator of an Internet town meeting to ask him the name of the president of India. When she obliged, he broke into his best smirk and said, "Vajpayee." Trouble is, Atal Behari Vajpayee is the *prime minister* of India. K. R. Narayanan is the president of India.[6]

But not all of Bush's mistakes are laughable. Some are deadly serious.

Bush Opposes the Comprehensive Test Ban Treaty

The Comprehensive Test Ban Treaty would limit the spread of nuclear weapons by preventing underground testing. Without the ability to test such weapons, it's difficult to imagine a nation gambling its very existence on using one.

In addition to most of America's key allies, the treaty was supported here at home by the current and former Joint Chiefs of Staff, thirty-two Nobel laureates in physics, dozens of Reagan and Bush military commanders and defense experts, and the directors of the three national nuclear laboratories.[7]

The United States was the first nation to sign the treaty, in 1996. It became the first nuclear state to fail to ratify it in 1999. Not long before the Senate—along party lines—voted against ratifying the Comprehensive Test Ban Treaty, Bush issued a statement opposing ratification.[8]

The opposition to the nuclear test ban treaty was led by North Carolina senator Jesse Helms (R-Tobacco) and Mississippi senator Trent Lott (R-Hair Spray), two of the finest minds of the twelfth century. After the treaty was killed, Lawrence Eagleburger, who served as secretary of state under President Bush and supported the treaty, criticized his fellow Republicans, saying, "I am afraid that some of the Republican leadership in the Congress is so anxious to embarrass the President because they dislike him so, that their tendency toward revenge, if you will, overwhelms their sense of what's in the national interest." When asked whom he blamed, Eagleburger said, "Well, there's no question that the Senate Majority Leader, amongst others, I think was clearly amongst those who was not prepared to let the President find a way out of this. . . . Let me put it this way: with regard to an awful lot of the Republicans in the Senate—it was not a time where they were prepared to demonstrate much political courage."[9]

The GOP Senate's failure to ratify the treaty deeply troubled America's closest allies. NATO members passed a resolution condemning the Senate's rejection of the CTBT. The resolution passed by the NATO Parliamentary Assembly says it was "deeply regretting that the United States Senate rejected ratification of CTBT." The Assembly also urged "the United States Senate to reconsider its position . . . as soon as possible."[10]

The British Parliament passed an Early Day Motion expressing "grave concern at the US Senate's rejection of the Comprehensive Test Ban Treaty . . . and hopes that the Senate will reconsider this decision." The motion was signed by 359 members of Parliament, a majority of the body.[11]

Other key allies such as Germany, France, and South Korea had all urged U.S. ratification. In fact, the leaders of Germany, France, and England wrote an op-ed in the *New York Times* calling for support of the treaty.[12] But to no avail.

The fallout has been severe. America lost valuable credibility in its effort to persuade India and Pakistan to back away from the brink of nuclear confrontation. "The initial impact will be catastrophic in terms of the U.S. ability to be taken seriously in international efforts to control the spread of nuclear weapons," said Rebecca Johnson, the editor of *Disarmament Diplomacy.* "The signal the rest of the world gets is that the United States prefers to engage in playground partisan politics rather than working with its allies on collective efforts at international security."[13]

Perhaps Secretary Eagleburger was right. Perhaps Republicans were so consumed with hatred for President Clinton they could not bring themselves to ratify this treaty—even though as the nation with the world's most sophisticated nuclear arsenal it is in our strong self-interest to limit other nations' ability to catch up to us technologically.

But whether the motive was vengeance or ignorance, the result was the same. George W. Bush played a role in harming American foreign policy. Imagine what he'd do if he became president.

Bush Dithered on Kosovo

On March 24, 1999, President Clinton launched air strikes against Serbian leader Slobodan Milosevic to stop the practice of "ethnic cleansing" in the former Yugoslavian province of Kosovo. Fully two weeks after the military engagement began, Bush was asked his position on Kosovo—the first large-scale NATO fighting in history. He said, "Uh, I support winning. And, uh, the strategy must—America must be slow to engage militarily, but once we engage, we must do so to win."[14]

Did you get that? W is for "Uh . . . winning." I suppose that's better than being for "Uh . . . losing." And it gets worse. Four months after his "Uh, I support winning" comment—and five months after the massive air strikes had begun, Bush still had to admit to a reporter that he didn't know where Kosovo is. "I do need somebody to tell me where Kosovo is," he said. "I know how to ask."[15]

Bush's dangerous ignorance seems to know no borders. Consider the following examples:

Pakistan

After flailing around trying to remember the name of the general who had initiated a coup in this nuclear-armed country, Bush said the coup, which overthrew a democratically elected government, was "good news for the subcontinent" because it would bring "stability to the country."[16] As the oldest constitutional democracy in the world, the United States of America is not in the habit of praising military coups overthrowing freely elected civilian authority.

And by the way, W, the general's name is Pervez Musharraf.

The Middle East

Bush declared that he intends to "stand by Israel. We're not gonna allow Israel to be pushed into the Red Sea." A neat trick given the fact that Israel borders the Mediterranean and barely touches the Red Sea. Bush went on to extol the virtues of what he called an "inter-ballistic missile system that intercepts missiles." But there's no such thing as an "inter-ballistic missile."

Chechnya

Even as he was cramming for his major foreign policy address in late 1999, Bush demonstrated staggering, embarrassing, avert-your-eyes ignorance. Reading from his own speech in an interview, Bush declared that the United States should take action in Chechnya "if the Russian government attacks innocent women and children." When asked if that was in fact happening now, Bush was clueless. Bush shouted to a foreign policy adviser: "They are attacking women and children, aren't they?" Then he returned to the phone and declared, "Condi Rice is shaking her head in agreement."[17] No, you dope, she's shaking her head in amazement that such a doofus could be a serious contender for the presidency. (Besides, don't folks *nod* their heads in agreement and *shake* their heads in disagreement?)

China

Bush darn near committed us to a war with the largest country in the world. In an interview with the conservative columnist Cal Thomas, Bush was asked if the United States should commit military power to prevent the People's Republic of China from forcibly taking Taiwan. "Yes," he replied bluntly. "What you're asking is should we honor the defense pact with Taiwan and the answer is yes."[18] Ever since Richard Nixon, American policymakers have followed what's called "strategic ambivalence" about our response to a Chinese attack on Taiwan; never directly saying it would mean war, never directly saying it wouldn't. The ambivalence has kept the Chinese off balance, and on the mainland, for over thirty years. Bush blew it in less than thirty seconds.

Bush later called Thomas back and tried to unscramble the eggs, saying, "It's important that all disputes over Taiwan and China be settled peacefully. The One-China policy has worked, allowing Taiwan to grow and maintain a strong market economy, which is a good example to Beijing."[19]

Condi Rice, you've got your work cut out for you.

Star Wars: The Sequel's Even More Expensive Than the Original

As dangerous as Bush's ignorance on foreign policy is, it's his blind faith in Star Wars that is most frightening. Since Ronald Reagan first called for it back in 1983, the United States has spent more time and more money (albeit not adjusted for inflation) on Star Wars than on the Manhattan Project (which invented the atomic bomb) and the ICBM program (which developed our long-range missiles) combined.[20]

This summer the Star Wars system failed yet another crucial test, as we, the taxpayers, ponied up $100 million to try to hit a bullet with a bullet. The rocket carrying the interceptor missile failed to deploy properly, and all was lost.

Perhaps that's why some fifty Nobel Prize winners, including twenty-one winners of the Nobel Prize in physics, have written an open letter asking our nation's leaders to abandon national missile defense. The Nobel laureates say it won't work, but it will be destabilizing, as Russia and China will embark on an arms race to overwhelm our missile defense. I know Bush is smart, but is he really smarter than fifty Nobel Prize winners?

One of the big issues here is "countermeasures"—the means by which our adversaries could defeat the national missile defense system. One way would be to overwhelm the system with decoys—perhaps even place a warhead inside a Mylar balloon and launch hundreds of decoy balloons. So far the system has been unable to discriminate against live and decoy targets.

And even comparatively poor countries could afford Mylar balloons. Can't you see it? The People's Republic of Guadador defeats America's multibillion-dollar Star Wars system by floating up hundreds of Mylar balloons! They could get creative and use those black "Over The Hill!" balloons made for people's fiftieth birthday, or they could be sweet and use those adorable Winnie-the-Pooh balloons. I'll bet there are even thousands of "Millennium 2000" balloons left over from New Year's Eve. The options are limitless, if you're creative.

Another problem with Bush's Star Wars plan is that rogue states may be more likely to fire short-range missiles, which are easier for them to develop and deploy, and which the proposed national missile defense won't be able to stop.

But despite these concerns, Bush seems to have such a total belief in Star Wars that he's willing to bet your life on it. He's so confident it will work that he's suggested unilateral reductions in America's nuclear arms.[21] He says that we'll be so safe under the Star Wars umbrella we can give away our arms without demanding corresponding cuts in the Russian or Chinese missile programs. But such a move would leave us in a world with more missiles in the hands of potential adversaries (whose only rational response to a Star Wars system that threatens to rob them of their own deterrent would be to build so many missiles they could overwhelm our missile defense). Hmmm. More missiles for our potential adversaries, fewer missiles in the U.S. arsenal, and only a dubious Star Wars system to defend us. Great thinking, W.

What's wrong with deterrence? Our adversaries have had nuclear weaponry for nearly a half-century, and we've never had a Star Wars system. They've never attacked because they've been deterred by massive response—massive retaliation, or suicide for a small country, Mutually Assured Destruction for a superpower. That system has kept the peace for two generations. Why not continue what we know works?

The truth is, Bush has been remarkably hazy about all of this. As the *New York Times* has written, "Neither Mr. Bush nor his aides would discuss his proposals in detail, leaving many questions about how—and whether—he could bring about a new era of arms control in a Bush Presidency."[22]

Bottom Line

The bottom line for Bush on foreign and defense matters is he's dangerously ignorant. As the great Texas populist and former agriculture commissioner Jim Hightower said about someone else, "If ignorance is bliss, he's the happiest man in America." But Bush's ignorance isn't funny. It could be enormously destabilizing. He has no idea who has their finger on the nuclear buttons in emerging nuclear powers. He has opposed sensible arms control treaties like the Comprehensive Test Ban Treaty, while supporting risky unilateral reductions in our own arms without demanding corresponding cuts from our adversaries—all because he still believes in a Star Wars fantasy that so far has only succeeded in destroying the budget.

In the last analysis, you should ask yourself: Can we really afford a president who thinks the G-8 is one of the coordinates in Battleship?

But I'm no longer laughing at the thought of a Bush presidency. I'm trying to raise kids on this planet.

chapter 14

Is Bush Really Dumb?
Or, "Let's Get Ready to STUMBLE!"

"Bush has a new campaign slogan. It's 'Reformer with Results.' Which I think is a big improvement on the old one: 'A Dumb Guy with Connections.' "

(David Letterman, *Late Night with David Letterman,* CBS)

"They finally found some dope in the Bush campaign. It's the candidate."

(Jay Leno, *The Tonight Show with Jay Leno,* NBC)

Knowing that I'm from Texas, that I've met Bush and am friendly with some of his top advisers, I get the question all the time. And I'm not sure how to answer it: Is Bush really dumb?

The very fact that the question is asked presupposes the answer. Or at least it suggests there's a valid issue as to whether W has the cranial capacity to lead the world.

My own sense is that Bush doesn't lack for potential; he's not limited by anything but his own laziness and lack of intellectual curiosity. He has a keen sense of politics, is an avid baseball fan, and strikes me as at least conversant on the issue of education reform. He's also a world-class b.s. artist—in the best sense of the word. He strikes me as the kind of guy you would love to chaw on a mess o' ribs with at the Salt Lick Barbecue in Driftwood, Texas.

But of course, all of that is, as my Texas friends would say, like telling your date, "You don't sweat much for a fat chick." Alexander Pope called it "damning with faint praise." (Pope was an English poet, Governor. Karl Rove will explain it to you.)

But beyond a basically pleasant disposition, however, Bush has shown little of the quality of mind we have a right to expect in a president. He doesn't seem to learn from his mistakes. Indeed, his ignorance is buttressed by his arrogance. When he was asked by the *New York Times* what he had learned from his primary challenge from John McCain he replied, "Nothing."[1]

When you watch the guy giving a speech, you get the sense he ain't getting' past the second round of *Who Wants to Be a Millionaire.* The feeling that if he went to a mind reader, they'd only charge half price. That if a thought wanted to cross his mind it'd need a canteen. You understand why, when he was in the oil business, folks said, "If air ever goes to $40 a barrel, I want the drilling rights to W's head."

The *Washington Post* did a major story on the issue of Bush's brains. The most damning material came from Bush's own friends, staff, and supporters:

- He can't even read ten whole pages of briefing material: "If there's a 10-page paper," says chief of staff Clay Johnson, Bush wants to know "what are the two pages that contain all the content?" (*Washington Post,* 1/19/00)

- Larry Lindsey, Bush's economics adviser, tries to spin Bush's ignorance as a sign of his security. "Sometimes he will blurt out in a meeting, 'Hey, Lindsey, run that by me again in English.' " (Ibid.) Great. Ignorance as a virtue.

- Peter Gebhard, a Harvard Business School classmate, damns his old pal with faint praise, telling the *Post:* "Was he the smartest guy in the class? No. Was he the dumbest? No. I guess he was like most of us who fell along that bell-shaped curve that I'd guess you'd call Harvard mediocrity." (Ibid.) There's a slogan for you: "Bush. Not the Dumbest Guy in the Class."

- Al Hubbard, another Harvard classmate, who is now a Bush campaign adviser, recalls that Bush sat silently in the back of the room. "That says it all," says Hubbard. "He was not trying to get a good grade." (Ibid.) You're right, Mr. Hubbard. It *does* say it all.

- Bush's great weakness, concludes Harvard professor Howard Gardner, a renowned expert in cognition and education, is what he calls "existential intelligence," meaning the capacity to ask and consider big questions. Who are we? What are good and evil? Will we survive or falter? What should we want from our lives? "So far," Gardner says, "W. seems to be clueless" in this mode of thinking. (Ibid.) Of course, this mode of thinking is exactly what the presidency is all about.

- Dr. Gardner concludes that "there is no evidence in any of [the primary] debates that he's digested . . . ideas, made them his own and is able to draw on them thoughtfully on his own. Even if he could take me to a library and show me he had checked out a thousand books, they didn't stick." Dr. Gardner believes that what's in doubt about Bush is not so much intelligence per se, but rather "intellectual laziness. I think throughout his life he has not done any more homework than he has to." (Ibid.)

- And here's what W himself had to say to the *Post*: "Intelligence is can you think logically," Bush explains. "Intelligence is do you have a basis from which to make decisions. Intelligence in politics is do you have good instincts." (Ibid.) Let's deconstruct that answer, shall we?

"Intelligence is can you think logically." Okay. Apparently it's not "can you speak grammatically," but we get your drift. Seems that you think intelligence and logical thought are connected. I'm with you so far. But it's a very thin standard, making no mention of creativity, which is at the heart of intelligence. Computers, after all, are logical. But they aren't intelligent.

"Intelligence is do you have a basis from which to make decisions." Again, Mr. Grammar is bedeviling us. But W seems to be asking—or perhaps asserting—that intelligence has something to do with the ability to collect, assess, and assimilate information in order to make deci-

sions. That's an even more cramped definition of intelligence than his previous statement limiting it to logical thinking skills. It's the kind of sentence that would have been edited out of one of those moronic self-help business books you see in the airport.

"Intelligence in politics is do you have good instincts." Good instincts? Instinct is innate. An instinct is an act utterly detached from intellect. A reflex is an instinct. The doctor hits your knee and your leg jumps. That doesn't make you Einstein. Intelligence cannot be defined as instinct or we're all lost. But perhaps that's why Bush is comfortable thinking of himself as bright even though he's never worked to develop his intellect. Judgment, which is at the heart of the kind of intelligence a president needs, requires work. It demands a restless, questing, seeking mind. Try saying that about Bush without laughing. W can settle back in his little mental La-Z-Boy because he thinks instinct is intelligence.

Bush has convinced himself that he can make good decisions based on the options and information he receives from those around him. That's dangerous for any leader; disastrous in a president. Such intellectual passivity would allow the staff, the bureaucracy, and the lobbyists to shape all W's decisions by controlling the information and options that are presented to him. I know. I've been there. President Clinton's mastery of policy and his breathtakingly broad reading habits kept everyone else off balance, and ensured he was at the top of the information pyramid. W would be a helpless, hapless victim of those who work harder, read more, and think creatively regardless of their agenda.

You're probably not surprised that I'm worried about Bush's capacity to succeed as president. But take a look at Bush in his own words (many of the best of these gems were compiled by Jacob Weisberg and posted on Slate.com as "Bushisms").

Warning: Reading too many of these in a row might make you dizzy.

"It's kind of rhetorical. I will be ready. But I feel ready. . . . 'I am ready' kind of means I'm ready when I swear in. You caught me." Answering a reporter's question about whether he's ready for the presidency.

(*Los Angeles Times*, 7/1/99)

"If you're sick and tired of the politics of cynicism and polls and principles, come and join this campaign."

> (Hilton Head, South Carolina, 2/16/00)

"I didn't do it in '88. I never have. Maybe I should." On whether he'd read his party's platform.

> (*Dallas Morning News,* 6/18/95)

"This is not my first trip to this incredible land called Silicon Valley. It's my first trip as President of the United States. Soon to be President of the United States." During a fund-raising trip to California.

> (*Washington Post,* 7/2/99)

"I was raised in the West. The west of Texas. It's pretty close to California. In more ways than Washington, D.C., is close to California." In Los Angeles.

> (*Los Angeles Times,* 4/8/00)

"Actually, I—this may sound a little West Texan to you, but I like it. When I'm talking about—when I'm talking about myself, and when he's talking about myself, all of us are talking about me."

> (*Hardball,* MSNBC, 5/31/00)

GOV. BUSH (TEXAS): Because the picture on the newspaper. It just seems so un-American to me, the picture of the guy storming the house with a scared little boy there. I talked to my little brother, Jeb—I haven't told this to many people. But he's the governor of—I shouldn't call him my little brother—my brother Jeb, the great governor of Texas.

JIM LEHRER: Florida.

GOV. BUSH: Florida. The state of the Florida.

> (*The NewsHour with Jim Lehrer,* PBS, 4/27/00)

"I'm gonna talk about the ideal world, Chris. I've read—I understand reality. If you're asking me as the president, would I understand reality, I do." On abortion.

> (*Hardball,* MSNBC, 5/31/00)

"States should have the right to enact reasonable laws and restrictions particularly to end the inhumane practice of ending a life that otherwise could live." Again on abortion.

(Cleveland, 6/29/00)

"You might want to comment on that, Honorable." To New Jersey's secretary of state, the Honorable DeForest Soaries, Jr.

(*Washington Post*, 7/15/00)

"Unfairly but truthfully, our party has been tagged as being against things. Anti-immigrant, for example. And we're not a party of anti-immigrants. Quite the opposite. We're a party that welcomes people."

(Cleveland, 7/1/00)

Bush: "First of all, Cinco de Mayo is not the independence day. That's dieciséis de Septiembre, and—"

Matthews: "What's that in English?"

Bush: "Fifteenth of September." (Dieciséis de Septiembre is the 16th of September, not the 15th.)

(*Hardball*, MSNBC, 5/31/00)

"You don't get everything you want. A dictatorship would be a lot easier." Describing what it's like to be governor of Texas.

(*Governing* magazine, 7/98)

"He has certainly earned a reputation as a fantastic mayor, because the results speak for themselves. I mean, New York's a safer place for him to be." On Rudy Giuliani.

(*The Edge with Paula Zahn*, 5/18/00)

"The fact that he [Gore] relies on facts—says things that are not factual—are going to undermine his campaign."

(*New York Times*, 3/4/00)

"I think we agree, the past is over." On his meeting with John McCain.

(Dallas Morning News, 5/10/00)

"You subscribe politics to it. I subscribe freedom to it." Responding to a question about whether he and Al Gore were making the Elián González case a political issue.

(In Palm Beach, Florida, as quoted by the Associated Press, 4/6/00)

"We want our teachers to be trained so they can meet the obligations, their obligations as teachers. We want them to know how to teach the science of reading. In order to make sure there's not this kind of federal—federal cufflink."

(At Fritsche Middle School, Milwaukee, 3/30/00)

"People make suggestions on what to say all the time. I'll give you an example; I don't read what's handed to me. People say, 'Here, here's your speech, or here's an idea for a speech.' They're changed. Trust me."

(Interview with the *New York Times,* 3/15/00)

"The senator has got to understand if he's going to have—he can't have it both ways. He can't take the high horse and then claim the low road."

(To reporters in Florence, South Carolina, 2/17/00)

"I'm very gracious and humbled."

(This Week, 2/20/00)

"I don't want to win? If that were the case why the heck am I on the bus 16 hours a day, shaking thousands of hands, giving hundreds of speeches, getting pillared in the press and cartoons and still staying on message to win?"

(Newsweek, 2/28/00)

"I thought how proud I am to be standing up beside my dad. Never did it occur to me that he would become the gist for cartoonists."

(Ibid.)

"I've changed my style somewhat, as you know. I'm less—I pontificate less, although it may be hard to tell it from this show. And I'm more interacting with people."

(Ibid.)

"This is Preservation Month. I appreciate preservation. It's what you do when you run for president. You gotta preserve." Speaking during Perseverance Month at Fairgrounds Elementary School in Nashua, New Hampshire.

(*Los Angeles Times,* 1/28/00)

"We must all hear the universal call to like your neighbor just like you like to be liked yourself." At a South Carolina oyster roast.

(*Financial Times,* 1/14/00)

"I can't remember any specific books." Bush's response to a child at Royal Elementary in Florence, South Carolina, who had asked him to name his favorite book as a child. The question was asked at an event in which Bush was highlighting his commitment to children's literacy.

(*Washington Post,* 8/27/99; *Dallas Morning News,* 8/27/99;
Sacramento Bee, 8/29/99)

"My education message will resignate amongst all parents."

(*New York Post,* 1/19/00)

"If you don't measure, if we're having to guess whether or not our children are learning, by the time it's too late we're going to find out that they're not, if they're not."

(Campaign speech, MSNBC, 2/15/00)

"A key to foreign policy is to rely on reliance."

(*Boston Globe,* 1/23/00)

'I think it's important for those of us in a position of responsibility to be firm in sharing our experiences, to understand that the babies out of wedlock is a very difficult chore for mom and baby alike. . . . I believe we ought to say there is a different alternative than the culture that is proposed by people like Miss Wolf in society. . . . And, you know, hopefully, condoms will work, but it hasn't worked."

(Meet the Press, 11/21/99)

"Put the 'off' button on." To parents bothered by the amount of profanty and violence on television.

(Associated Press, 2/15/00)

"The important question is, How many hands have I shaked?" Answering a question about why he hasn't spent more time in New Hampshire.

(New York Times, 10/23/99)

"An economically vile hemisphere." Describing half the world.

(Newsweek, 2/28/00)

"It was just inebriating what Midland was all about then."

(From a 1994 interview, as quoted in *First Son*, by Bill Minutaglio)

What Others Have Said About Bush and His Brain

[Bush's] scripted and vague answers continue to raise questions about his readiness to be president."

(Associated Press, 12/8/99)

[Bush's opponents signaled that] perhaps the most vigorous line of attack against him will be that he lacks the intellectual heft and poise to lead the country," indicated rivals Senator John McCain, Senator Orrin Hatch, and Alan Keyes.

(New York Times, 12/8/99)

[Bush's debate] performance lacks the gravitas that a lot of people have come to associate with the presidency," said Marvin Kalb, executive director of Harvard University's Shorenstein Center on the Press, Politics and Public Policy.

(*Boston Globe*, 12/8/99)

"Bush, all lightness of being, struggles to be viewed as serious enough for the job."

(*Time*, 11/15/99)

"The fear continues to fester about Bush . . . that at 53 he has the same cavalier attitude toward knowledge that he had at 21: he could learn what he needs to know, but he doesn't think it's worth his time."

(*Time*, 11/15/99)

"The larger issue . . . is whether the son of the former president, who admits that he became serious about life only after his 40th birthday, has the requisite depth and solidity to be an effective president."

(Shapiro, *USA Today*, 11/11/99)

If you think the media left of Rush Limbaugh is some sort of liberal conspiracy, I defy you to explain the following two statements:

"George W. Bush says as little as possible, positive or negative, since every time he ventures down from Mount Platitude, his QQ (Quayle Quotient) goes up another click."

(James Pinkerton, conservative columnist and former senior aide to President Bush, *Philadelphia Inquirer*, 1/10/00)

Bush's demeanor suggests "an atmosphere of adolescence, a lack of gravitas—a carelessness, even a recklessness, perhaps born of things having gone too easily so far. . . . Bush is taking a political party along on his ride. He and it will care if on November 7, 2000, people think of him as an amiable fraternity boy, but a boy."

(George F. Will, *Washington Post*, 8/11/99)

The Bottom Line

Bush is worse than dumb. He's lazy, arrogant, and defiantly ignorant. He clearly has an adequate God-given intellect, but because everything's been handed to him on a silver platter (usually by a butler) he's never developed it. Call me crazy, but I think age fifty-three is a little late to start—and the White House is the wrong place for remedial education.

chapter 15

Cheney Mania! Poppy's Pick

"It's the Wizard of Oz ticket: Cheney needs a heart and Bush needs a brain."

> (Jay Leno, *The Tonight Show with Jay Leno*, 7/25/00)

"I obviously thought about the record. And this is a conservative man. So am I."

> (George W. Bush, endorsing Dick Cheney's voting record in Congress, *Washington Post*, 7/28/00)

Poppy's Pick

The normally deft Bush spin operation was remarkably ham-handed in explaining the choice of former Bush defense secretary Dick Cheney as W's running mate. That's because W and Poppy seem to have cooked this one up on their own. Of all the people in the world W could turn to for advice, he had to go to the guy who'd made the worst running mate selection in the twentieth century.

I wonder if W has, as the headshrinkers say, "issues" regarding his dear old dad. Even on the verge of his nomination for the presidency, Bush whined to ABC's Peter Jennings that he'd "inherited half his friends and all his enemies."[1] And even now, his father seems more stunned than proud when he ponders his son's success. In an interview with the *New York Times* not long before the GOP convention, former President Bush was perhaps too candid, expressing more amazement than pride at his son's success: "I'm amazed—still amazed—at the way he's done," he said.[2]

It may be that behind every successful man is an amazed father, but I doubt it.

Perhaps I'm reading too much into this. But I can't get out of my mind an encounter I had with W. I had accompanied President Clinton to the opening of the George Bush Presidential Library in College Station, Texas. The day was beautiful, the former president and first lady were gracious, President Clinton was generous in his praise. But when W noticed that President Clinton had been joined by Garry Mauro, W's opponent for the upcoming 1998 gubernatorial campaign, the governor blew a gasket.

He let me know in no uncertain terms, one Texas politico to another, that he was angry. He was hotter than a two-dollar pistol: eyes flaring, language coarse. Now, I don't mind a politician with a temper. Lord knows Bill Clinton has one. And my wife doesn't call me "Potty Mouth" for nothing. So none of that bothers me in the least. But it's always instructive to see what sets a guy off. W went ballistic, I think, not so much because the Democrat he was about to trounce was there, but because Bill Clinton was there. *President* Bill Clinton. Standing right alongside Poppy, W's hero, whom Clinton had not merely beaten; he'd humiliated.

I feel for W. I really do. But does he have to use his vice presidential selection to suck up to his father? Couldn't he have gone into therapy, or onto *Oprah*, or written a tell-all book, *Poppy Dearest*?

Irresponsible?

When Dick Cheney's name was first leaking out of the Bush camp, I thought it was a diversion. I said so on television, adding that choosing Cheney would be irresponsible, given his history of serious medical conditions. My friends who support W jumped ugly with me. But I was right. The Cheney choice is still being digested by the body politic, but it looks like it's already giving my Republican friends heartburn.

Pop Quiz: Which of these medical maladies has Dick Cheney NOT had:

A) A heart attack;

B) Another heart attack;

C) A third heart attack;

D) Open-heart, quadruple-bypass surgery;

E) Cancer;

F) Gout;

G) An allergic reaction to a pomegranate that nearly killed him;

H) The heartbreak of psoriasis.

If you guessed "H" you're our lucky winner! Of course, we don't really know, since as of this writing, the Bush-Cheney ticket won't release Cheney's medical records.

What's the matter, W: Couldn't find someone who'd only had *two* heart attacks? This guy doesn't need to be on the ticket, he needs to be on *E.R.*

My favorite example of the Bush campaign's Orwellian desire to control language is how all of W's spinners mindlessly repeat the adjective "mild" before "heart attack." Know what the definition of a "mild" heart attack is? One somebody else has. Of course, the ever helpful Poppy got the venerable Houston heart surgeon Dr. Denton Cooley to vouch for Cheney's health—even though Cooley had never examined Cheney. I know Cooley is a great doctor and all, but can he really assess someone he's never examined? If so, when it's time for my next physical, I'm just gonna call my doctor, so I can turn my head and cough over the phone.

After Cooley had spoken with Cheney's doctor and released a statement declaring, "Mr. Cheney is in good health with normal cardiac function," Cheney's real cardiologist, Dr. Jonathan Reiner, issued a correction saying he had not, in fact, given Cooley quite such a glowing report, noting he "did not characterize him as having normal cardiac function."[3]

Oops. That "not" is a pretty big three-letter word. As Mark Twain once said, "the difference between the right word and the nearly-right word is the difference between a lightning bolt and a lightning bug." Looks like this is more of a lightning bolt.

But, obviously, even his worst political adversaries wish Secretary Cheney nothing but the best of health. As troubling as Cheney's many heart problems are, I'm even more bothered by the lack of heart he showed as a congressman.

Cheney in Congress: He Put the "Wreck" in Record

On the day Dick Cheney was publicly asked to join Bush's ticket, his former colleague Newt Gingrich thought about their salad days together in Congress: hurting old people, screwing poor people, harming hungry children. Ahh, Newt must have thought, those were the good old days. But then it came over Newtie that Cheney was not quite like him. And, as he confided to the *Washington Times:* "Cheney's voting record was slightly more conservative than mine."[4]

More conservative than Newt Gingrich? That's like being more pompous than Rush Limbaugh; like being more weird than Dennis Rodman. But it's true. Cheney's voting record is distinctly more conservative than Newt's (which is no mean trick, since Newt basically wants to return to the feudal system). And perhaps because of his upbringing on the rugged and lonely Wyoming prairie, Cheney was remarkably comfortable being on the losing end of some of the most lopsided votes. Of the 435 members of the House, many of them from very conservative districts, Cheney was frequently one of just a dozen or two who staked out the kookiest of the kook-right positions.

Plastic Guns for Terrorists and Armor-Piercing Bullets for Cop-Killers

No other area shows the sheer lunacy of Dick Cheney's voting record better than guns. In 1988, Cheney was one of only four members of the entire House of Representatives to oppose the Undetectable Firearms Act of 1988, which outlawed guns that are made with so little metal they can defeat a metal detector.[5] When he was asked to defend a vote that was so right-wing even the National Rifle Association didn't support it, Cheney's smart-aleck response was, "Well, obviously I wasn't in the pocket of the NRA."[6] Jeez! Maybe not, Dick, but only because you're farther out on the fringe. But take heart, Dick. I'll bet that vote wins you "Legislator of the Year" from the International Brotherhood of Terrorists.

Perhaps trying to suck up to that all-important cop-killer vote, Cheney was one of only twenty-one House members to oppose a ban on armor-piercing "cop-killer" bullets.[7] And almost as inexplicably, he was one of just thirty-one congressmen to vote against funding programs to prevent family violence and to provide shelter for the victims of family violence.[8]

Women and Children First

Donna Brazile, Al Gore's provocative campaign manager, got in hot water a few months back when she said the GOP "would rather take pictures with hungry people than feed them." But how else can you explain W's constant photo ops with children, and his enthusiastic embrace of his running mate's all-out war against children?

There are few government programs as universally beloved as Head Start. Except by Dick Cheney. Even when 400 or more of the 435 members of the House were voting in support of Head Start, Dick was a lonely voice of opposition. In 1984, Cheney was one of only ten members of the entire House to oppose a bill to allow Head Start to continue to exist for another two years.[9] In 1986, he was one of only twenty-seven members of the House to vote against funding Head Start for the next four years.[10]

And it's not like Cheney had some odd, idiosyncratic burr under his blanket about Head Start. He has a consistent record of opposing programs to help children, especially poor, hungry children.

Cheney was one of only eight House members to vote against a health bill that allowed the National Health Service Corps and the federal immunization program to continue operating.[11] As a rugged individualist, Cheney must have thought those kids could give themselves their own doggone immunizations.

The same with school lunches. Cheney voted against the school lunch and child nutrition programs at least ten times, including votes against reauthorizing the school lunch program, which has been remarkably successful in fighting childhood hunger, votes against cost-of-living adjustments for the program, and votes against expanding eligibility for the program.[12] Darn tootin', Dick. It's about time somebody stopped those freeloading children from gorging themselves on those free school lunches.

After Bush picked him to be his running mate, and the fertilizer started hitting the ventilator, Cheney lamely suggested—are you ready for this?—"I could find some [votes] I might tweak and do a little bit differently."[13] Tweak, Dick? Tweak? That's like Jack the Ripper saying he might want to "tweak" a few of those London hookers. He didn't "tweak" 'em, he slashed 'em. And that's what Dick the Ripper did to Head Start and children's nutrition programs. Tweak my aunt Fannie.

Cheney's other line of defense is, "I think that was also the 1980s. . . . Today we are in a different era. We've got a surplus."[14] And why is that, Dick? We had a deficit in the 1980s because people like you voted for the Reagan tax cuts for the rich.

I love this. First Cheney helps create the deficit. Then he blames the deficit for his votes to cut Head Start and child nutrition programs. That's like the guy who murdered his parents, then threw himself on the mercy of the court because he was an orphan. And, yes, Dick, we do have a surplus now. Wanna guess why? Because the American people bounced your ass and the rest of the Bushies out in 1992, and let Bill Clinton and Al Gore put the economy back on track.

Cheney's opposition to children doesn't end when they're young. He tried to hurt them at every chance he got. He was one of just a handful of House members to vote to kill the college student aid programs—both in 1985 and 1986.[15] (As someone who was educated on federally guaranteed student loans, I'm glad he failed.) He also opposed the creation of the Department of Education—twice—and voted against adult education, against bilingual education, against pretty much any kind of education.[16]

His defense today is that he does not believe that "anything with 'education' on it is good.' " [17] Now we know why Cheney wanted to be on Bush's ticket: he's pro-ignorance.

Civil Rights? Not Our Dick

Cheney's record on civil rights and racial justice is no better than his sorry record on education. In one of his most infamous votes, Cheney in 1986 voted against a resolution expressing the sense of the House that the president should urge the South African government to negotiate with the country's black majority, grant immediate and unconditional release to Nelson Mandela and other political prisoners, and recognize the African National Congress as a legitimate representative of the black majority. [18]

Nowadays, Cheney says he voted against the resolution not because he didn't want to free Nelson Mandela, but because "there was a big debate over the best leverage we could use to get Nelson Mandela free." [19] Oh? And voting *against* a resolution calling on the brutal apartheid regime to release him was the best leverage we had to get Mandela released?

Cheney also says—now—that he voted against the Free Mandela Resolution because he opposed unilateral sanctions and supported Reagan's policy of "constructive engagement." [20] That's mendacious in the extreme. The Free Mandela Resolution was silent on the issue of sanctions. [21] Cheney is correct when he says he opposed sanctions on the apartheid regime. He did oppose standing up to that infamously racist regime—once again showing himself to be on the wrong side of history. Multinational sanctions played a key role in the ultimate collapse of apartheid, the freeing of Mandela, and the peaceful transfer of power to President Nelson Mandela. But of course, if Dick Cheney had had his way, the racist thugs might still be in power, and Nelson Mandela might still be in prison.

Cheney was no friendlier to civil rights legislation closer to home. He repeatedly voted against civil rights programs in the 1980s. He opposed even allowing a floor vote on a bill that sought to ensure application of four major civil rights laws. He voted against overriding

President Reagan's veto of the Civil Rights Restoration Act of 1987, which provided broad coverage of four civil rights laws: Title IX of the Education Amendments of 1972; Section 504 of the Rehabilitation Act of 1973; the Age Discrimination Act of 1975; and Title VI of the Civil Rights Act of 1964.[22] And he voted against even collecting data on hate crimes—attacks based on race, religion, sexual orientation, or ethnicity.[23]

And in case you ladies thought Dick was on your side, he also voted against the Equal Rights Amendment.[24] Apparently full equality for women was an idea whose time had not yet come for Mr. Cheney. In his defense, Cheney says he opposed the ERA because he feared it would require that women be drafted.[25] Hey, Dick: we haven't even drafted any *men* for twenty-five years. But at least he's consistent: Cheney was so opposed to the draft during the Vietnam War that he got several deferments. He never spent a day in uniform himself, but he was eager to ship my cousin Dennis (a Marine sniper) off to Kuwait to do Cheney's fighting for him.

"Let Them Eat Dog Food"

I'll say this for Cheney: he's consistent. Just as he was consistently opposed to women, children, and civil rights, Cheney was also tireless in his quest to cut Social Security, and anything else that might help seniors. In 1981, our man Dick was one of only twenty members of the House who voted against restoring minimum Social Security benefits. In 1983, Cheney backed raising the normal Social Security retirement age from sixty-five to sixty-seven. In 1985, Cheney was one of only thirty-nine members of the House who backed a budget that limited cost-of-living adjustments for Social Security to 2 percent annually for three years.[26]

Cheney was one of only twelve House members to vote against the Older Americans Act Amendments of 1984, which provided nutrition and support services for elderly people. He also voted against funding it for three years after that.[27]

Sure, anybody can pander to the old and the infirm. But it takes a gutsy guy—a real Mountain Man; a real Dick, if you will—to hurt the most vulnerable people in our society. But it was either them or the defense contractors and, you know, it's only business, Granny.

The Environment

Although he represented one of the most beautiful states in the union, Cheney was no tree-hugger. He was one of only sixteen House members who opposed continuing the Endangered Species Act.[28] The Endangered Species Act, by the way, is one reason you can still see bald eagles swooping through the skies of Wyoming. But what do they contribute to society anyway?

Maybe you're not a "species environmentalist." But unless you're in favor of more toxic waste, you're going to find it difficult to understand why Cheney voted at least five times against measures to continue, expand, or strengthen the Superfund hazardous waste cleanup program.[29] Or why Cheney voted seven times against authorizing clean water programs, like the Safe Drinking Water Act and the Clean Water Act.[30]

My grandpa Begala used to say, "You eat a peck of dirt in your life; it won't hurt you." But I don't think Grandpa B was thinking about eating toxic waste. And I can't imagine what Dick Cheney was thinking about when he voted against cleaning it up. (If you want the full story on his voting record, check out www.bush-cheney.net.)

And You Thought the Lincoln Bedroom Was Bad

Dick Cheney has a well-deserved reputation for probity. But if a recent press report is to be believed, he may have stumbled while at the Pentagon. The Associated Press, citing "documents gathered by congressional fund-raising investigators," has reported that "long before there were White House coffees for Democratic donors, Dick Cheney entertained major Republican contributors at private meetings at the Pentagon. . . . Cheney was host for at least two GOP donor gatherings inside the Defense Department in 1991 and in 1992, the records show."[31]

Given the thorough and careful vetting that Poppy gave Cheney, I'm sure W knew all about this. Just spare us the pious lectures about returning decency to the White House, would you?

The Bottom Line

What is it, something in the Bush genes? The vice presidential selection is the first presidential decision. And, just like Poppy, W royally screwed up. It's not that Cheney is incompetent, it's that Bush is. Either Bush knew that Cheney had more ailments than a dog has fleas and picked him anyway (in which case he's irresponsible) or he didn't properly check the man for annoying maladies like cancer and heart attacks (in which case he's, well, irresponsible).

The same with Cheney's Looney Tunes voting record. (It's a cartoon reference, Karl. Bush will explain it to you.) Either Bush knew about the terrorist guns and cop-killer bullets and Nelson Mandela votes and picked him anyway (see above parenthetical judgment) or he didn't even check the guy out. Poppy told him whom to pick, and he obeyed.

Either way, Bush now has one presidential decision on which we can judge him, and thousands of nutball congressional votes he's embraced. Bush says he's happy with his choice of Cheney. Not half as happy as I am, W.

Afterword

How fitting.

The guy who got into Yale despite being an underachieving party boy, the guy who got into the Texas Air National Guard despite scoring in the bottom 25 percent of the pilot aptitude test, the guy who got into the oil business despite not knowing a dry hole from a dry martini, the guy who got into the owners' box of the Texas Rangers despite owning less that 2 percent of the team, the guy who got into the multimillionaires' club despite being a failure in business now gets into the White House despite losing the election.

I always knew rich kids could get Daddy's lawyers to get them out of trouble, but this is ridiculous.

Yes, Al Gore lost his home state—and that's embarrassing. But how much more embarrassing is it that Bush lost his home country?

For the 50,158,094 of us who voted for Al Gore, this book is an "I Told You So." For the 49,820,518 of you who voted for George W. Bush, this book is filled with uncomfortable, but carefully documented, facts. For the 445,343 of you who voted for Pat Buchanan, this book is for your next bonfire. And for the 2,783,728 of you who voted for Ralph Nader, this book is a thank-you note.[1] When Jerry Falwell starts picking our Supreme Court justices, we have no one but the Naderites to thank.

While avowedly partisan, I hope this book has also been something of a public service: I've gathered the pre-presidential Bush record into one tidy, helpful handbook, so you can get to know our new president in all his wonderful contradictions: ignorant, yet arrogant; with a sense of entitlement matched only by his sense of aggrievement; an anti-intellectual whose most important issue is education; a Christian who signs death warrants for mentally retarded men and elderly women.

But the most glaring contradiction is between the image of Bush as a conciliator and the real Bush—a hard-nosed combatant whose temper is so nearly out of control that he was literally on the verge of a fistfight on the very night he was also on the verge of the presidency. The night before the election, someone asked Bush if he still did an impression of the *Dallas Morning News'* Wayne Slater, the reporter who revealed that Bush had lied when he denied having been arrested. Bush claims the conversation Slater reported never took place. So at the mention of Slater's name, Bush's face flushed. He waved his finger in the reporter's face and hissed, "I can do an imitation of that conversation he made up."

Bush cocked his fist back with such force he knocked a wineglass out of a reporter's hand. Referring to Slater as a bodily function, he expressed a willingness to go "mano a mano" with the reporter. Slater later said he believed Bush had been joking, but one eyewitness to the incident told me Bush seemed unmistakably angry, and that the uniter was ready to divide Mr. Slater from his front teeth.[2]

If this is how Bush responds to gentle ribbing on what should have been one of the best days of his life, what's he going to do when he faces real pressure as president? Well, if his conduct during the election contest is any indication, he'll break out in a boil and hide on his ranch, emerging only often enough to lie about whether Dick Cheney has had another heart attack.

Maybe my friend Don Imus was right. He supported Bush because he thought W would be a much better source of material. (In fairness to Mr. Imus, it should also be noted he thought Al Gore was the single most evil man on the planet. But that's only because Don doesn't count himself.)

W's ascension to the presidency is rich with history. Barbara Bush will now have the honor of being the first woman to be both the wife and the mother of failed presidents.

It is also rich with irony. The candidate who slimed John McCain in the primaries and smeared Al Gore in the general election is now the president who pledges to elevate the nation's tone and bring civility to our discourse. Kind of like Michael Corleone brought peace to the mob by killing the heads of the other four families.

But perhaps the better movie metaphor is from Junior's favorite character in his favorite movie: Bluto, the John Belushi character in *Animal House.* At the end of the movie, we're told what became of the main characters after they left Faber College. Bluto was the self-destructive, hard-drinking, toga-partying lead animal in the house. Years later, he is "Senator John Blutarsky of Pennsylvania."

Even in the movies they couldn't imagine him as president.

Sources

Title page

1. *Special Report with Brit Hume*, 1/11/00.

chapter 1

1. *Calgary Sun*, 3/12/00.
2. *U.S. News & World Report*, 5/7/00.
3. *New Republic*, 4/10/00.
4. Associated Press, 8/18/99; UPI, 8/18/99; *Newsweek*, 8/16/99, 8/7/00; Bush affidavit signed on July 20, 1999; *Austin American-Statesman*, 5/16/99; *Sacramento Bee*, 4/23/00.

chapter 2

1. *Dallas Morning News*, 7/4/99.
2. *Boston Globe*, 5/23/00.
3. *Chicago Tribune*, 1/18/00.
4. *Los Angeles Times*, 7/4/99; *Austin American-Statesman*, 7/17/99.
5. *Los Angeles Times*, 7/4/99.
6. *Boston Globe*, 5/23/00.
7. Ibid.
8. Ibid.
9. Ibid.
10. *Newsweek*, 7/17/00; Associated Press, 7/4/00.
11. Press conference, Tuscaloosa, Alabama, 6/23/00.
12. Associated Press, 6/24/00.
13. Ibid.
14. Ibid.

15. Ibid.

16. *Boston Globe,* 5/23/00.

chapter 3

1. *Weekly Standard,* 2/10/97.

2. No, I don't speak Chinese. I got this from David Quan, my old law school roommate, who consulted his sister-in-law, Sylvia, who was born in Hong Kong and is fluent in both Mandarin and Cantonese. "Lien" is Mandarin for "bush." Thanks, DQ.

3. Lubbock *Avalanche-Journal,* 10/26/78, 4/30/78; *Washington Post,* 7/30/99; George Bush for Congress Committee FEC report, 1/25/78.

4. Ivins and Dubose, *Mother Jones,* March/April 2000.

5. *Rolling Stone,* 8/5/99.

6. *Dallas Morning News,* 9/28/94; *Houston Post,* 10/9/94.

7. Ivins and Dubose, *Mother Jones,* March/April 2000.

8. Ibid.

9. Ibid.

10. Ibid.

11. *Dallas Morning News,* 5/7/99, 7/30/99.

12. *Dallas Morning News,* 5/7/94.

13. Ivins and Dubose, *Mother Jones,* March/April 2000.

14. Ibid.

15. *Dallas Morning News,* 7/30/99.

16. Ivins and Dubose, *Mother Jones,* March/April 2000, citing *Time,* 1991.

17. *Dallas Morning News,* 7/30/99.

18. *Time,* 10/28/91.

19. Ivins and Dubose, *Mother Jones,* March/April 2000.

20. Ibid.

21. *Wall Street Journal,* 1990, quoted in ibid.

22. *U.S. News & World Report,* 3/16/92.

23. Center for Public Integrity, 4/4/00; *Dallas Morning News,* 5/7/94.

24. Ivins and Dubose, *Mother Jones,* March/April 2000.

25. *Wall Street Journal,* 4/4/91.

chapter 4

1. *Austin American-Statesman,* 8/1/99.
2. *Fort Worth Star-Telegram,* 7/11/99.
3. *Houston Post,* 1/5/95.
4. *Baltimore Sun,* 3/28/00.
5. Texas Education Agency, 1998–1999 State AEIS report, www.tea.state.tx.us/perfreport/aeis/99/state.html.
6. *Chronicle of Higher Education,* 6/23/00.
7. Ibid.
8. *Washington Post,* 5/20/99.

chapter 5

1. National Economic Council, 7/00.
2. Ibid.
3. *National Journal,* 1/16/99; National Economic Council, 7/00.
4. *New York Times,* 8/6/00; Citizens for Tax Justice, 5/17/00, www.ctj.org.
5. millionairesforBush.com—a Web site sponsored by the Democratic National Committee.
6. Congressional Budget Office.
7. Calculated by millionairesforBush.com Web site.
8. *Dallas Morning News,* 6/21/99; *Abilene Reporter-News,* 6/22/99; CNN, 5/13/99.
9. *Dallas Morning News,* 1/27/00.
10. United Press International, 7/10/00.
11. *Houston Chronicle,* 7/11/00; CNN, 7/12/00; Associated Press, 7/11/00.
12. Citizens for Tax Justice Web site.
13. Ibid.
14. *74th Legislature Overhauls Tort Law,* House Research Organization, Session Focus No. 74-13, 6/3095; *Los Angeles Times,* 7/14/99.
15. *Los Angeles Times,* 7/14/99; *New Republic,* 8/16/99; *Washington Post,* 2/10/00.

16. *New Republic*, 8/16/99; *Texas Lawyer*, 12/23/99; *Los Angeles Times*, 7/14/99.
17. *Washington Post*, 2/10/00.
18. *New Republic*, 8/16/99; *New York Times*, 6/7/99; *Washington Post*, 2/10/00.
19. *Los Angeles Times*, 7/14/99.
20. *Dallas Morning News*, 6/22/99.

chapter 6

1. *Dallas Morning News*, 8/27/95, 5/11/95, 12/23/97, 5/27/99.
2. Texas Administrative Code, Title 22, Part 4, Chapter 89, Rule 89.7.
3. *Houston Chronicle*, 5/30/97.
4. *Houston Chronicle*, 3/23/99; *Greensboro News & Record*, 11/29/98.
5. Text of House Bill #2909.
6. *Austin American-Statesman*, 5/28/96.
7. *Houston Chronicle*, 4/27/99.
8. *Fort Worth Star-Telegram*, 5/22/99.
9. *Dallas Morning News*, 5/27/99.
10. *Washington Post*, 6/22/99; *New York Times*, 6/21/99.
11. *Good Morning America*, ABC, 5/10/99.
12. Associated Press, 2/14/00.
13. *Washington Post*, 3/3/00.
14. *San Antonio Express-News*, 5/19/99.
15. *Dallas Morning News*, 5/27/00.
16. *Portland Press Herald*, 6/6/99; Associated Press, 7/22/99.
17. *Portland Press Herald*, 6/6/99; www.vpc.org//resource/content/bush.htm; *International Defense Review*, 9/1/97; *Guns & Ammo*, 8/83; Bushmaster Products catalogue; Associated Press, 7/22/99.
18. *Houston Chronicle*, 12/9/99.

chapter 7

1. *Time*, 2/21/00.
2. Bush 7/15 SEC filing; letter from Exxon representative, 6/12/97; *Austin*

American-Statesman, 6/10/98; "Dirty Air, Dirty Money," June 1998 report by Texans for Public Justice, Center for Responsive Politics, www.crp.org.; *Grandfathered Air Pollution: The Dirty Secret of Texas Industries,* 4/27/98; Center for Responsive Politics, www.crp.org; Associated Press, 4/30/99.

3. *Portsmouth Herald,* 6/12/99; *San Antonio Express-News,* 4/14/99.

4. *Houston Chronicle,* 10/12/99.

5. *Houston Chronicle* (online version), 5/4/99; *Dallas Morning News,* 4/11/99, 4/12/99, 5/4/99; Associated Press State and Local Wire, 1/20/99.

6. *Austin American-Statesman,* 7/26/95, 6/10/98; *Houston Chronicle,* 11/19/97; Associated Press State and Local Wire, 1/20/99; "Dirty Air, Dirty Money," June 1998 report by Texans for Public Justice, Center for Responsive Politics, www.crp.org; *Grandfathered Air Pollution: The Dirty Secret of Texas Industries,* 4/27/98.

7. *Houston Chronicle,* 11/12/99.

8. *Houston Chronicle,* 11/9/99.

9. *Dallas Morning News,* 10/20/99; *Austin American-Statesman,* 10/20/99; *Fort Worth Star-Telegram,* 10/20/99.

10. *Dallas Morning News,* 3/12/99.

11. League of Conservation Voters, *2000 Presidential Profiles: George W. Bush,* 1/13/00.

12. Ibid.

13. *Fort Worth Star-Telegram,* 10/20/99.

14. *Texas Monthly,* 6/99.

15. *Austin American-Statesman,* 12/12/96.

16. *Ethnic NewsWatch,* 1/27/99.

17. *Dallas Morning News,* 1/3/99; *The Clean Air Act: New EPA Air Quality Standards—Implications for Texas,* Texas Legislative Council, 10/98.

18. TX PEER, Superfund a Super Deal, www.txpeer.org/bush/Superfund3 .html.

chapter 8

1. *Houston Chronicle,* 5/17/00.

2. *New York Times,* 5/17/00.

3. Associated Press, 5/17/00.

4. *Dallas Morning News,* 5/15/00.

5. *New York Times,* 5/17/00.

6. *This Week,* ABC, 7/16/00.

7. General Accounting Office, Barbara Bovbjerg, associate director, Income Security Issues, 4/22/98.

8. Cordes and Steurle, *A Primer on Privatization,* Urban Institute, 11/99.

9. *Wall Street Journal,* 5/12/00.

10. Center for Budget and Policy Priorities, 5/12/00; *Wall Street Journal,* 4/21/00; *Washington Post,* 5/11/00.

11. Associated Press, 5/17/00.

12. *Atlanta Journal and Constitution,* 5/16/00.

13. *Wall Street Journal,* 6/22/00.

14. *Newsweek,* 6/25/00.

15. *Meet the Press,* 11/21/99.

16. Testimony of Kilolo Kijakazi, Center for Budget and Policy Priorities, House Ways and Means Committee, 2/10/99.

17. "Summary of a New Study on Winners and Losers from 'Privatizing' Social Security," Testimony Submitted to the Social Security Subcommittee of the Commerce Ways and Means, House of Representatives, 3/3/99.

18. *Inside Politics,* CNN, 5/15/00.

19. *Washington Post,* 5/16/00.

20. Ibid.

chapter 9

1. Associated Press, 8/24/99.

2. Texas Legislature Online, www.capitol.state.tx.us.

3. Steve Rosenthal, AFL-CIO interview with Brit Hume, *Fox Special Report,* 5/11/00.

4. Center for Public Policy Priorities, *Working but Poor: A Study of the Forgotten Texans Who Work Hard Yet Remain in Poverty,* 3/99; *National Journal,* 8/7/99; *Austin American-Statesman,* 12/19/99.

5. Bush campaign event, "The Door," East Baltimore, Maryland, 7/14/99.

6. Economic Policy Institute, *The Next Step: The New Minimum Wage Proposals and the Old Opposition,* 3/8/00.

7. Associated Press State and Local Wire, 3/25/99; *San Antonio Express-News,* 4/23/99.

8. *Dallas Morning News,* 11/26/97; *Corpus Christi Caller-Times,* 3/18/97.

9. *Amarillo Daily News,* 2/7/97.

10. Texas Legislative Council, *Summary of Enactments, 76th Legislature,* 1999.

11. Texas Legislative Council, *Summary of Enactments, 75th Legislature,* 1997; *Texas Lawyer,* 6/30/97.

12. *Austin American-Statesman,* 9/10/97; *Dallas Morning News,* 5/27/95, 9/26/95.

13. *Houston Chronicle,* 9/2/99.

14. Texas Department of Economic Development, "About Texas" fact sheet, www.tded.state.tx.us/TXoverview; Office of the Governor, Appointment Division, 2/11/99; Texas State Auditor's Office, "An Audit Report on the Department of Economic Development," 1/24/00; *Journal of Commerce,* 6/5/97.

chapter 10

1. Bush Web site, *www.georgewbush.com.*

2. *Texas Monthly,* 8/95.

3. *Medical Economics,* 12/22/97; *Houston Chronicle,* 5/23/97.

4. Associated Press, 7/16/99; *Los Angeles Times*/CNN, 7/14/99; *Washington Post,* 7/16/99.

5. *Washington Post,* 4/25/99; *Wall Street Journal,* 3/17/99.

6. Letter from Richard S. Foster, Office of the Actuary, Health Care Financing Agency, to House Ways and Means Health Subcommittee minority staff, 2/23/00.

7. *New York Times,* 3/17/99.

8. *Fox Sunday News,* 1/30/00.

9. *Los Angeles Times,* 6/6/00.

10. *Why Seniors Need Access to Affordable Prescription Drugs,* U.S. House Democratic Policy Committee, 4/14/00.

11. *National Journal,* 4/1/00.

12. *Los Angeles Times*, 6/6/00.

13. U.S. Census Bureau report on health insurance coverage, 10/99.

14. George W. Bush interview in Manchester, New Hampshire, with WMUR, 11/10/99.

15. *New York Times*, 4/11/00.

16. *New York Times*, 2/18/00.

17. *Austin American-Statesman*, 2/26/99; *Dallas Morning News*, 12/2/98.

18. Associated Press State and Local Wire, 3/11/99; *Houston Chronicle*, 3/28/99; *Austin American-Statesman*, 2/26/99.

19. *New Republic*, 7/12/99.

20. *Dallas Morning News*, 8/15/99.

21. Ibid.

22. Families USA press release, 4/11/00.

23. Families USA fact sheet on medical savings accounts, 2/22/00.

24. Testimony of Consumers Union Health Policy Analysis director Gail Shearer before the House Democratic Health Working Group, 7/22/98.

chapter 11

1. *Boston Herald*, 11/18/99.

2. *Dallas Morning News*, 8/11/99; *Fort Worth Star-Telegram*, 8/13/99.

3. *Washington Post*, 8/16/99.

4. *Fort Worth Star-Telegram*, 8/13/99; *Washington Post*, 8/16/99.

5. *Washington Post*, 8/15/99.

6. Republican debate, Los Angeles, CNN, 3/2/00.

7. Shapiro, *The Nation*, 4/7/97; Elliott and Ballard, *Texas Lawyer*, 2/26/96; Death Penalty Information Center Web site.

8. Shapiro, *The Nation*, 4/7/97; O'Brien, op-ed, *Washington Post*, 5/28/97; *Good Morning America*, ABC, 5/4/97; Aron, *USA Today*, 12/7/98; Elliott and Ballard, *Texas Lawyer*, 2/26/96; Death Penalty Information Center Web site.

9. CNN, 6/25/95, 3/31/96; Elliott and Ballard, *Texas Lawyer*, 2/26/96; Bendavid, *Texas Lawyer*, 8/14/95; Ballard, *Texas Lawyer*, 4/17/95; Death Penalty Information Center Web site.

10. *U.S. News & World Report,* 8/10/99.

11. *New York Times* (editorial), 6/17/99.

12. *Houston Chronicle,* 6/21/99; *Dallas Morning News,* 6/26/99.

13. *Houston Chronicle,* 6/5/99.

14. *Fort Worth Star-Telegram,* 6/4/99.

15. Associated Press, 6/22/99.

16. *Fort Worth Star-Telegram,* 6/22/99.

17. Associated Press, 5/29/97; *Washington Post,* 11/7/97; *Houston Chronicle,* 12/15/97; Texas Coalition to Abolish the Death Penalty; *San Antonio Express-News,* 1/23/00; http://www.tdcj.state.tx.us/statistics /stats-home.htm.

18. Pacifica News Service, 6/25/99; *San Antonio Express-News,* 1/23/00.

19. *San Antonio Express-News,* 9/2/96; Associated Press, 9/1/96; *Houston Chronicle,* 1/19/95, 1/19/95.

20. *Dallas Morning News,* 4/14/99.

21. *New York Times,* 8/7/00.

22. *Dallas Morning News,* 6/1/00.

23. *Reno Gazette Journal,* 6/2/00.

24. Interview with Deece Eckstein, Senator Ellis's chief of staff, 5/31/00.

25. *Atlanta Journal,* 6/23/00.

chapter 12

1. *Austin American-Statesman,* 5/18/99.

2. *Washington Post,* 3/24/99.

3. Bill Minutaglio, *First Son,* pp. 99–100.

4. Associated Press, 1/31/00, 2/4/00; *Palm Beach Post,* 2/4/00.

5. *Newsweek,* 2/28/00.

6. *Chicago Tribune,* 6/4/92.

7. *National Catholic Reporter,* 4/9/82.

8. *The Tax Lawyer,* Winter 1984; *World News Digest,* 5/27/83.

9. *Larry King Live,* CNN, 3/3/00.

10. Associated Press, September 11, 1987.

11. http://www.bju.edu/aboutbju/president/.

12. *The Christian Century,* May 5, 1993.

13. Republican primary debate, Lexington, South Carolina, MSNBC, 1/7/00.

14. Associated Press, 4/6/00.

15. Ibid.

16. Ibid.

17. *Austin American-Statesman,* 4/11/00, 4/12/00.

18. Ibid.

19. *Houston Chronicle,* 4/23/00.

20. Associated Press, 4/22/00; *Houston Chronicle,* 4/23/00.

chapter 13

1. Knight-Ridder News Service, 10/11/99.

2. *National Journal,* 4/3/99.

3. *Boston Globe,* 6/6/99.

4. *Austin American-Statesman,* 3/19/00.

5. *Wall Street Journal,* 3/2/00.

6. *New York Times,* 2/26/00.

7. *New York Times,* 10/6/99; *As It Happens,* Canadian Broadcasting Corp., 10/14/99; *Christian Science Monitor,* 10/13/99; Coalition to Reduce Nuclear Dangers backgrounder, 9/14/99; *Albuquerque Journal,* 6/11/99.

8. *New York Times,* 10/14/99; Agence France Presse, 10/6/99.

9. *As It Happens,* Canadian Broadcasting Corp., 10/14/99; *Hartford Courant,* 10/5/97; *Star Tribune* (Minneapolis-St. Paul), 6/4/99; *Washington Post,* 10/14/99.

10. Reuters, 11/15/99; Resolution on the Comprehensive Test Ban Treaty, NATO Parliamentary Assembly, 11/15/99.

11. Early Day Motion 929, 10/20/99.

12. *Newsweek,* 10/18/99; Agence France Presse, 10/14/99.

13. *Straits Times* (Singapore), Branson op-ed, 10/16/99.

14. Interview, *Inside Politics,* CNN, 4/7/99.

15. *Manchester Guardian Weekly,* 8/25/99.

16. Interview with Andy Hiller, WHDH-TV, 11/4/99.

17. Associated Press, 11/17/99.

18. *Washington Times,* 7/19/99.

19. *National Journal,* 7/8/00.
20. *Wall Street Journal,* 5/24/00.
21. *New York Times,* 5/24/00.

chapter 14

1. *New York Times,* 3/17/00.

chapter 15

1. Transcript of interview posted online, 7/29/00, abcnews.go.com/onair /WorldNewsTonight/wnt000728_PJBush_feature.html.
2. *New York Times,* 7/8/00.
3. *New York Times,* 7/25/00.
4. *Washington Times,* July 25, 2000.
5. *1988 CQ Almanac,* p. 40-H, vote #118.
6. *New York Times,* 7/28/00.
7. H.R. 3132, vote #1465, 12/17/85.
8. *1984 CQ Almanac,* p. 6-H, vote #14.
9. *1984 CQ Almanac,* vote #238.
10. H.R. 4421, vote #2384, 9/16/86.
11. *CQ Almanac,* 1987, House Vote #404, passed 401–8, 11/3/87.
12. H.R. 7, vote #1312, 9/18/85; *1984 CQ Almanac,* p. 24-H, vote #66; p. 32-H, votes #93 and #94; *1985 CQ Almanac,* p. 88-H, vote #274; p. 90-H, votes #280, #281, #282, and #283; *1983 CQ Almanac,* p. 114-H, vote #387; vote #1309, 9/18/85.
13. *Washington Post,* 7/27/00.
14. Ibid.
15. *1985 CQ Almanac,* vote #391.
16. *1979 CQ Almanac,* votes #289 and #468; *1983 CQ Almanac,* vote #335; *1984 CQ Almanac,* pp. 493–494, vote #290; *1984 CQ Almanac,* vote #292; *1987 CQ Almanac,* votes #304, #305.
17. *New York Times,* 7/28/00.
18. *1986 CQ Almanac,* p. 86-H, vote #304.
19. *New York Times,* 7/28/00.

20. Ibid.

21. *1986 CQ Almanac,* p. 86-H, vote #304.

22. *1984 CQ Almanac,* p. 74-H, vote #233; S. 557, vote #2041, 3/22/88; *1983 CQ Almanac,* 16-C, vote #14; *1983 CQ Almanac,* p. 52-H, vote #162.

23. H.R. 3193, vote #2138, 5/18/88.

24. *1983 CQ Almanac,* p. 16-C, vote #14.

25. *New York Times,* 7/28/00.

26. *1983 CQ Almanac,* p. 10-H, votes #20 and #22; H.R. 152, vote #1124, 5/22/85; *1981 CQ Almanac,* p. 62-H, vote #178. He also voted to cut $13 billion in Medicare funding from the sick and the aged in 1984 (Bush-Cheney.net).

27. H.R. 4785, vote #2355, 8/8/84; *1984 CQ Almanac,* p. 96-H, vote #317.

28. *1987 CQ Almanac,* vote #492.

29. *1984 CQ Almanac,* p. 98-H, vote #323; p. 102-H, vote #333; *1985 CQ Almanac,* p. 124-H, vote #394; p. 128-H, vote #409; *1986 CQ Almanac,* p. 116-H, vote #408.

30. *1981 CQ Almanac,* p. 86-H, vote #266; *1984 CQ Almanac,* p. 16-H, vote #45; H.R. 3282, vote #2267, 6/26/84; *1986 CQ Almanac,* p. 34-H, vote #110; *1985 CQ Almanac,* p. 72-H, vote #226; *1985 CQ Almanac,* p. 72-H, vote #225; *1987 CQ Almanac,* p. 2-H, vote #8; p. 8-H, vote #14.

31. Associated Press, 7/26/00.

Afterword

1. All vote totals from *Washington Post,* 12/1/00.

2. *Houston Chronicle,* 11/8/00; author interview with eyewitness, 12/12/00.

About the Author

Paul Begala, former counselor to President Clinton, is the co-host of MSNBC's *Equal Time*. He first gained national prominence as half of the political consulting team of Carville & Begala. He served as a senior strategist to the 1992 Clinton-Gore campaign, and has helped run political campaigns across America and in several foreign countries. He helped John F. Kennedy, Jr., found *George* magazine, where he was one of the original contributing editors. He has also written articles for *Esquire* and the *Washington Monthly,* and opinion columns for the *New York Times* and the *Los Angeles Times Magazine.* He is also a research professor of government and public policy at Georgetown University.

TALKING POINTS: THE CASE AGAINST GEORGE W. BUSH

1. Bush Will Screw Up the Economy

- He squandered Texas' record surpluses on tax cuts for the more affluent—now Texas faces a budget shortfall.
- Bush wants to give nearly $2 trillion of your surplus in tax breaks for the rich.
- Bush's tax plan gives the richest 1 percent a $50,000 a year tax cut—60 cents a day for most working families.

2. Bush Is a Threat to Social Security

- Experts say Bush's plan to privatize part of Social Security will cut benefits by 20 to 54 percent—even his chief economic adviser says guaranteed benefits will be cut.
- Bush says he's open to raising the retirement age.
- His risky plan takes out nearly $1 trillion from Social Security and could lead to an S&L-style bailout.

3. Bush Is Hazardous to Your Health (Care)

- Bush bitterly opposed extending the Children's Health Insurance Program to 200,000 more kids, but passed a $45 million tax break for Big Oil.
- Bush's health care plan has been called a "shell" and covers less than 10 percent of the uninsured.
- Bush opposes a real Patients' Bill of Rights and doesn't spend a dime to help millions of middle-income seniors afford prescription drugs.
- Bush said that some people choose to be uninsured.

4. Bush Made Texas Tops in Air Pollution

- Bush let corporate polluters help write environmental rules, which required only "voluntary" compliance.
- In 1999 Houston overtook Los Angeles as the "smog capital" of the U.S.
- He's worked hand-in-hand with chemical companies to undermine public safety.

5. Bush Claims Credit for Education Improvements That Came Before Him

- The *Fort Worth Star-Telegram* says: "Education experts, and even Bush aides, say that his predecessors are more responsible for improvements in Texas education."
- Reductions in class size, standardized testing, and teacher accountability were all in place before W became governor.
- Bush's education plan drains much-needed funds from public schools, leaving kids trapped in failing schools. He also said "higher education is not my priority."

6. Bush Is in Bed with the Gun Nuts

- Bush signed an NRA-backed bill to allow Texans to carry guns in church, amusement parks, nursing homes, and hospitals.
- The NRA says if Bush wins, they'll be working out of the White House.

7. Bush Is Not Coming Clean About Where He Was During the Vietnam War

- Bush received preferential treatment to get into the Texas Air National Guard.
- He only scored in the 25th percentile in the pilot aptitude test, yet received a special commission to be a pilot—despite a long waiting list.
- His commanding officer says he failed to report for duty for an entire year.

8. Bush Was a Failure as a Businessman

- Bush traded on his family name and contacts to get into the oil business in Texas.
- He was such a bad businessman his company was nicknamed "El Busto."
- He was made managing partner of the Texas Rangers. He traded Sammy Sosa.

9. His First Big Decision? Dick Cheney

- Cheney voted against banning plastic guns that can get past metal detectors.
- He voted against banning cop-killer bullets.
- He voted against reauthorizing Head Start, school lunches, and the immunization program.

10. (Shhhhhhh: He's Not the Sharpest Knife in the Drawer)

- The very fact that everyone is asking whether Bush is smart enough to be president is a pretty good sign he ain't.
- See the title of this book (which is a direct quote from W).